P9-EDL-457

# KOREA

## *A Land Divided*

*by Carol Farley*

Dillon Press, Inc.   Minneapolis, Minnesota  55415

Library of Congress Cataloging in Publication Data

Farley, Carol J.
  Korea, a land divided.

  (Discovering our heritage)
  Summary: Describes the history, geography, customs, family
life, school life, sports and games, and folklore of Korea. Also
discusses the problems created by the split of the north and
south into two nations, the communist Democratic People's
Republic of Korea and the anticommunist Republic of Korea.
  1. Korea—Juvenile literature.  [1. Korea]  I. Title. II. Series.
DS907.4.F37      1983          951.9               83-7789
ISBN 0-87518-244-5

© 1983 by Dillon Press, Inc. All rights reserved

Dillon Press, Inc., 500 South Third Street
Minneapolis, Minnesota 55415

Printed in the United States of America
  2  3  4  5  6  7  8  9  10  91  90  89  88  87  86  85  84

J
951.9
Farley

*The photographs are reproduced through the courtesy of
Byron Clendening, the Chicago and New York offices of the
Korean Cultural Service, and the Korean National Tourism
Corporation in Chicago.*

# Contents

# Fast Facts About South and North Korea

|  | **South Korea** | **North Korea** |
|---|---|---|
| **Official Name:** | *Taehan-minguk* ("Republic of Korea"). | *Choson-minjujuui-inminkonghwaguk* ("Democratic People's Republic of Korea"). |
| **Capital:** | Seoul. | P'yŏngyang. |
| **Location:** | South Korea occupies the southern half of the Korean peninsula, which extends south from northeastern China. | North Korea occupies the northern half of the Korean peninsula, which extends south from northeastern China. |
| **Area:** | 38,025 square miles (98,484 square kilometers), including islands, but not the 487 square miles (1,262 square kilometers) of the demilitarized zone; South Korea stretches 300 miles (480 kilometers) from north to south and 185 miles (298 kilometers) from east to west; it has 819 miles (1,318 kilometers) of coastline. | 46,540 square miles (120,538 square kilometers), including islands, but not the 487 square miles (1,262 square kilometers) of the demilitarized zone; North Korea stretches 370 miles (595 kilometers) from north to south and 320 miles (515 kilometers) from east to west; it has 665 miles (1,070 kilometers) of coastline. |
| **Elevation:** | *Highest*—Halla-san (Mount Halla), 6,398 feet (1,950 meters) above sea level; *Lowest*—sea level. | *Highest*—Paektu-san (Mount Paektu), 9,003 feet (2,744 meters) above sea level; *Lowest*—sea level. |
| **Population:** | *Estimated 1983 Population*—39,275,000; *Distribution*—55 percent of the people live in or near cities; 45 percent live in rural areas; *Density*—1,033 persons per square mile (399 persons per square kilometer). | *Estimated 1983 Population*—19,291,000; *Distribution*—60 percent of the people live in or near cities; 40 percent live in rural areas; *Density*—414 persons per square mile (160 persons per square kilometer). |

|  | South Korea | North Korea |
|---|---|---|
| **Form of Government:** | Officially a constitutional republic, but political power is centralized in the country's president, who receives strong support from the military. | Officially a constitutional republic, but political power is held by the country's Communist Party, called the Korean Workers' Party. |
| **Important Products:** | Barley, beans, potatoes, rice, wheat; chemicals, machinery, processed foods, textiles; anthracite, iron ore, salt, tungsten. | Barley, corn, rice, wheat; chemicals, iron and steel, machinery, textiles; copper, iron ore, lead, tungsten, zinc. |
| **Basic Unit of Money:** | Won. | Won. |
| **Major Language:** | Korean. | Korean. |
| **Major Religions:** | Buddhism; Confucianism; Christianity. | The religious beliefs of many North Koreans include elements of Confucianism and Buddhism. |
| **Flag:** | Red and blue circle flanked by three bars at each corner. | Red star set in a white circle which is bordered by red and blue horizontal stripes. |
| **National Anthem:** | "Aegug-ka" ("National Anthem"). | No official anthem; "Aegug-ka" ("National Anthem") used as unofficial national anthem. |
| **Major Holidays:** | New Year's Day (January 1); Buddha's birthday (the eighth day of the fourth lunar month); Tano (the fifth day of the fifth lunar month); Ch'usŏk (the day of the full moon in the eighth lunar month); Liberation Day (August 15). | May Day (May 1); National Day (September 9). |

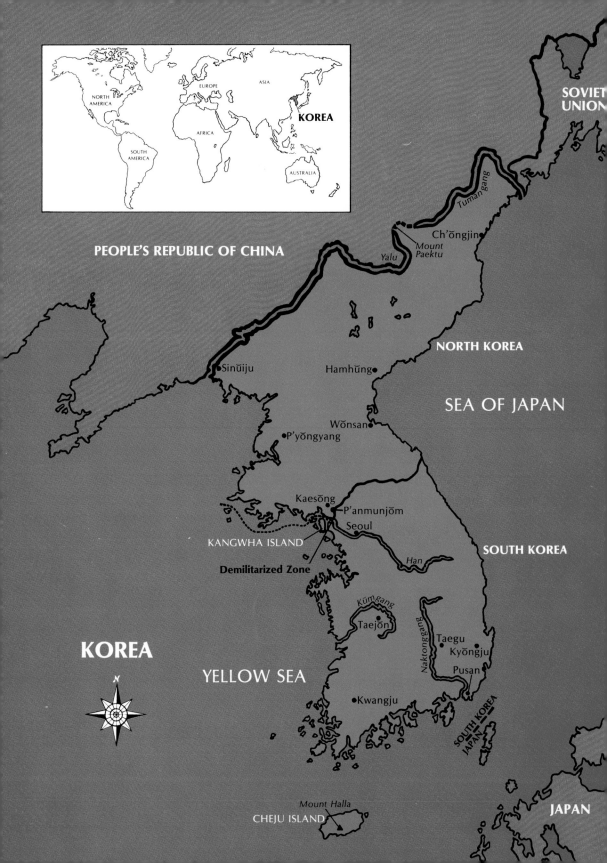

PEOPLE'S REPUBLIC OF CHINA

SOVIET UNION

NORTH KOREA

SEA OF JAPAN

SOUTH KOREA

JAPAN

KOREA

YELLOW SEA

NORTH
AMERICA

SOUTH
AMERICA

EUROPE

AFRICA

ASIA

KOREA

AUSTRALIA

Tuman-gang

Ch'ŏngjin

Mount
Paektu

Yalu

•Sinŭiju

Hamhŭng•

Wŏnsan•

•P'yŏngyang

Kaesŏng

P'anmunjŏm

Seoul

KANGWHA ISLAND

Demilitarized Zone

Han

Kŭmgang

Taejŏn•

Naktonggang

Taegu•
Kyŏngju•

Pusan•

•Kwangju

SOUTH KOREA
JAPAN

Mount Halla

CHEJU ISLAND

# 1. The Hermit Kingdom

For many years Korea was called the Hermit Kingdom because nobody knew very much about it. It was a mysterious peninsula—a piece of land sticking out into the water—not far from the northeast coast of the People's Republic of China. The country did not want visitors. Just as hermits like to live alone, it seemed that the Koreans wanted to live alone, too.

Until the nineteenth century, few Westerners knew anything about the Koreans or their country, and the people there were not interested in learning about the rest of the world. During its long history, Korea had been invaded by the Chinese, the Mongols, the Manchus, and the Japanese. Its rulers finally decided that since neighbors could not be trusted, Korea must cut itself off from the rest of the world. Like a hermit, Korea stopped talking to other countries.

Sometimes shipwrecked sailors would be tossed ashore on the coast or on one of Korea's many islands, for the country has water on three sides. If the sailors were Westerners, the Koreans kept them captive because they were so different looking. They were amazed to see that the Westerners had beards and large noses. In the distant rural areas, people said that Westerners had such long noses that they had to tuck them behind their ears when they drank.

A sailor from The Netherlands, Henrik Hamel, was captured in 1653 and held for almost fourteen years. The book he wrote about his adventures can still be read today. In his own time people wondered if his strange stories about Korea could be true. The Koreans did not believe his tales about the West either. They thought that Westerners were all barbarians, or savages.

Now, however, things have changed. Today Korea is eager for worldwide friendships, and the people are happy to share ideas with visitors. Today we Westerners know the secrets of the Hermit Kingdom because the Koreans are proud to talk about their long history. We know what life was like hundreds of years ago and what it is like today.

Imagine for a few moments that you are a shipwrecked sailor living in the year 1450. How did you get to Korea, and what did you find when you arrived? How was it different from today?

Maybe your ship was really sailing towards Japan, which is Korea's nearest ocean neighbor. The two countries are only 123 miles (206 kilometers) apart. You could have been sailing in the Yellow Sea, the East China Sea, or the Sea of Japan, all part of the

Pacific Ocean. Perhaps one of the many Koreans fishing off the country's east coast picked you up. Or perhaps you were able to swim to one of the 3,000 islands surrounding the coasts of Korea.

The weather in Korea was the same in 1450 as it is today, with four separate seasons. Because the country is at the far end of the world's largest continent, Asia, the climate is influenced more by the land than by the ocean. Seasonal winds called monsoons make the weather very hot in the summer and very cold in the winter. A shipwrecked sailor could not live long in the freezing water of the winter, so we will pretend that you reached Korea in the spring and stayed there as the seasons passed.

The spring is short—usually less than three months—but it is welcome after the long winter. In northern Korea winter may last six months. Winter in southern Korea is milder, but there is ice and snow for at least three months. The swallows return to all of Korea in March, and in April the cherry blossoms and forsythia bloom.

Mild spring days soon turn to very hot summer days. Often it is very rainy, too. Hot, wet weather is good for growing rice. Hundreds of years ago, as today, Korea was covered with bright green rice paddies during this season. Then, as now, people hoped that the rain would not come too fast or too hard

*Rice has been one of Korea's most important crops for hundreds of years. This farmer is sitting next to one of the paddies in which the rice is grown.*

because the rivers could overflow their banks and cause floods. There could also be typhoons, or hurricanes, near the coasts. You, as a sailor, would know how dangerous typhoons could be.

But in the fall the weather is usually good. The days are sunny and dry, and the sky seems especially clear and blue. "High sky" the Koreans call it. In October, which is called the "golden month," farmers harvest their rice. People lay bright red peppers out in the sun to dry, and they chop up onions and cabbage.

Hundreds of years ago the Korean people prepared food for the winter much as they do today.

The rivers and mountains probably looked much the same then as they do today. Korea is a mountainous country, sometimes called the Switzerland of Asia. Diamond Mountain, in North Korea, is famous for the beauty of its 12,000 rocky peaks. Long ago the Prince of Sweden visited there and said, "God spent six days creating the universe—He must have spent the seventh creating Diamond Mountain."

Korea's mountains have always provided fine homes for many wild animals. In the past, tigers roamed through them. Today the tigers are gone, but there are many wolves, foxes, deer, and beavers. There were many forests before modern warfare stripped some mountains of their timber, but young forests are growing on them again now.

Korea is almost the size of the state of Utah. Yet because it is so hilly, some Americans have said that if the many mountains could be ironed out the country would be larger than Texas. But Koreans of the past and of the present like their beautiful mountains just the way they are.

Some of these mountains were formed by volcanoes, but there are no active volcanoes anymore. The tallest mountain in Korea is Mount Paektu, located in the far north. Cheju Island has the highest and

most popular mountain in the south—Mount Halla.
Perhaps we could pretend that, like Henrik Hamel,
you were shipwrecked on the coast of this island.
Even hundreds of years ago Cheju was famous for its
mountains, its fishermen, and its horses. Today it is
famous for women divers and citrus fruits, too.

Rivers have always played an important role in
Korea. They have been natural boundaries, and they
have served many of the people's needs. Today, in the
north, the Yalu and the Tumangang rivers form a
border between Korea and China. Part of the Tumangang River also separates Korea from the Soviet
Union. The Han, the Kŭmgang, and the Naktonggang rivers flow south and empty into the East China
Sea or the Yellow Sea.

In 1450 the rivers were most important for trans-
portation. The major čities were built along their
banks so that people could move quickly by boat
from one place to another. Fishermen harvested a
steady supply of food from them, and farmers carried
their water to use on crops. But in the past there was
always great danger from flooding when the mon-
soon rains fell during the summer months.

Today an ancient sailor would be surprised to see
how modern science has harnessed the power of Korea's rivers. Dams have been built in both the north
and the south, and they help provide flood control

*Mount Halla, located on Cheju Island, is the highest mountain in the southern part of Korea.*

and hydroelectric power. Rice paddies can be irrigated scientifically. There is still some flooding during very heavy rainfall, but the danger is not as great as it once was.

The Koreans would have looked the same in 1450 as they do today, with dark hair and dark, almond-shaped eyes. Because they were cut off from the rest of the world, they did not mingle with people of other nations, and only one race developed. Their skin is lighter in tone than that of the Japanese and not as yellow as that of the Chinese. They are taller than both these peoples. Since they rarely traveled far from home, they thought all the people of the world looked exactly like them. This is the reason they were so amazed to see strange-looking foreigners.

In 1450 the Koreans' clothing was very different from what they wear today. The wealthy people wore beautiful brocade robes. The common people dressed in white trousers, skirts, and jackets. Unmarried men and women wore no hats, but after marriage the men wore hats, and some women wrapped white cloths around their heads. Other women pulled their hair into knots at the back of their necks, and then put long, large hairpins through the knots.

Today most Koreans dress exactly the way you dress. But they still have colorful costumes, and they wear them on special days. All-white clothing is not popular in modern Korea; it is worn only by women in mourning.

The cities are very different now, too. In 1450 Seoul was the country's capital. Today it is still the capital of South Korea, while P'yŏngyang has become the capital of North Korea.

During the late fourteenth century, the king had walls built around Seoul to protect his palace and court. But just as you are too big to wear the clothing made for you years ago, Seoul grew too big to stay within these walls. Over eight million people live in the city today. The ancient walls are still there, but Seoul has grown far beyond them in every direction.

All over Korea the cities are growing larger. In the past, most Koreans were farmers or fishermen, and they lived in small villages. Now many of them live in busy cities and have jobs in industry. Some help to build ships, while others work in oil refineries and chemical factories. Still others mine coal, iron, and tungsten. And many people work in the textile factories. Look at the clothing you are wearing. Some of it was probably made in Korea.

Not long ago, a World Bank report said that Korea's economic growth is one of the outstanding success stories of recent times. Koreans are proud of this success. But even though the people work hard, they are not wealthy because war has made their

*Over eight million people live in Seoul, the capital of South Korea.*

country very poor. They have had peace for thirty years now, so they are slowly overcoming their poverty. But people still worry about war.

And this worry is the saddest difference between the Korea of the past and Korea today. In 1450 Korea was one country, united under one king, with one government for all. Today Korea is divided, the northern half of the country ruled by one government, and the southern half by another. The northern half is called the Democratic People's Republic of Korea, and the southern half the Republic of Korea.

The Koreans are still one people, with the same language, way of life, and traditions, but now their governments are enemies. Most Korean people feel very sad about this situation. They say that large, powerful countries have always caused their problems. Again and again over the centuries, they have been invaded by foreign armies. The twentieth century has been the most difficult of all.

Japan conquered the whole peninsula in 1910 and set up a Japanese government. When Japan lost World War II, the Allied forces came to Korea. They divided the country in half, near the thirty-eighth parallel of north latitude that you'll find on a map. Troops from the Soviet Union occupied the northern half, and soldiers from the United States the southern one.

*P'anmunjŏm has been the site of many important political discussions.*

In 1948 the United Nations (UN) sent a group to Korea to set up an election so that the Korean people could choose their own leaders. The talks about the election were held on the thirty-eighth parallel at a place called P'anmunjŏm. The Communist government in the north said that there was no need for an election there, and none was held. In the south, the people elected representatives who chose a president to head the Republic of Korea.

In 1950 troops from North Korea invaded South

Korea. For three years there was terrible fighting between the two countries, and soldiers helping each side died. Seoul and P'yŏngyang, the two capitals, were both nearly completely destroyed.

Many people from many lands suffered and died in the Korean War. Over a half-million soldiers from the United States, Canada, and fourteen other UN countries fought on the side of the South Koreans. Forty-one other UN members gave military equipment or food and other supplies to South Korea. The People's Republic of China sent over three-quarters of a million troops to help the North Koreans, who also received military aid from the Soviet Union.

Perhaps one of your grandparents took part in this war, one of the bloodiest in history. Nearly two million soldiers were killed or wounded in the fighting. In addition, about a million ordinary South Koreans lost their lives, and several million were made homeless.

Peace talks begun by the United Nations ended the Korean War in 1953. The North Koreans, the People's Republic of China, and the Soviet Union spoke for one side. The South Koreans and sixteen members of the United Nations spoke for the other side.

These peace talks are still going on in the 1980s, and the uneasy truce, or cease-fire, that was agreed to by the two sides still exists. Foreign armies are still in Korea helping each of the two governments. The Korean people cannot freely travel between the north and the south. Some families are divided, and they cannot get messages to each other. Soldiers stand on either side of a special cease-fire zone, watching to see that no one goes across. Sometimes there is trouble in or near this zone.

Despite this sad division, the Koreans are proud of their land, and they want the world to know the good things about it. The biggest difference between the Koreans of 1450 and the Koreans of today, then, is that today they eagerly welcome visitors. Only a few country people are surprised to see Westerners now. They may be curious about different-colored skin or hair, but they make sure that Westerners feel welcome.

Koreans are eager to show visitors how modern they are. They will show you their universities, their factories, their arts and crafts centers, their sports arenas, and their museums. They will take you to their zoos and their flower gardens. Their cities are full of new buildings, skyscrapers, and fast subways.

The people of Korea are eager to share their heritage, or treasure from the past, too. They will show you temples, paintings, and ornaments that were made centuries ago. Even though Korea is

*Beautiful temples are one of Korea's many treasures from the past.*

rapidly emerging into the modern industrial world, its people have not forgotten their beautiful old objects and traditions.

A shipwrecked sailor of long ago would have been eager to hurry home to tell everyone about the strange new country he had lived in. Today you would be eager to tell people about Korea, too. A mixture of the ancient and the modern, it is a land in which exciting things are happening.

No one calls Korea the Hermit Kingdom today. Now visitors sometimes call it by a very ancient name, the Land of the Morning Calm, because it is so quiet and beautiful in the morning sunshine.

Most Koreans are glad that their land is calm and peaceful now. They hope that one day they will be united under one government again, but they have not been able to agree as to which government should rule the whole peninsula.

# 2. Make It Korean

Some countries are called melting pots because so many races of people live together peacefully. Korea has only one race of people, but it is a melting pot of ideas. Because powerful countries have invaded their land many times, the people have been forced to listen to new ideas. If they liked the ideas, they fit them into their own lives. They made them Korean.

This blending of ideas has made modern Koreans the way they are today. In the past, ideas from China, India, and Japan were blended together to make Korean ways which still exist today. Since 1945, when Korea was divided, the north has blended ideas about government from the Soviet Union with those of its own. The south has done the same thing with ideas from the Western nations.

Although the governments of the two Koreas are very different, the people still have many of the same ways. In all of modern Korea, the family is the most important part of daily life. Koreans do not see themselves as people standing alone; they see themselves as parts of one large family. When a Korean man introduces his wife, he does not say "my wife," he says "our wife." When she introduces her mother, she says "our mother." The success or failure of one family member brings success or failure to the whole family.

Korean young people feel that they must always obey their parents. The father is especially respected, and his advice is always sought. In 1981 Korean young people were asked this question: "Do you want to choose your own husband or wife, or do you want your parents and a matchmaker to choose for you?" More than seventy percent of both males and females answered that they wanted their families to choose for them.

Most Koreans can trace their families back for hundreds of years. Foreigners joke that there are only five Korean families—the Kims, the Yis, the Parks, the Hans, and the Chungs. This is not true. There are more than two hundred different family names, but these five are the most common.

When Koreans write or give their full names, the family name comes first. The next name is a generation name, chosen by the head of the clan to give to all children who are born in that generation. The third name is chosen by the two parents. For example, a Korean boy might be named Kim Yong Tu. When the generation name and given name are put together, they sometimes have a special meaning. Yong Tu, for instance, means Dragon Head. When other members of the Kim family meet Yong Tu in future years, they

*No matter what family they come from, all children are important in Korea.*

will know what generation he was born in. Sometimes the place of a family's first home is also mentioned in a name. The Taegu Kims came from Taegu.

In olden times girls had no given names. They received their father's name and were called his daughter. Today they are given names which also may have some meaning. Ok Cha, for instance, means Jade Child.

Women keep their father's name all their lives. That is why Mr. Kim's wife might be called Mrs. Park. When they have a child, Mr. Kim and Mrs. Park will be called "Yong Tu's father" and "Yong Tu's mother."

All married people hope to have a son because the eldest son will carry on the life of their family and care for them in their old age. Yet they value daughters, too, because every child is important in Korea. In fact, the Koreans say that "children are king in Korea" because they love them so much.

Friends are important, too. On the streets of Korea you will see young men holding hands. They think of each other as brothers and act as if they were almost part of the same family. Young women hold hands and behave the same way. But boys and girls rarely touch each other in public. They feel that males should stay with males and females with females until marriage. Some modern young people are trying to change this old idea, but very few of them have dates during their teenage years.

Koreans believe that all old people belong with their families. They are surprised that Westerners have homes for the elderly. When Koreans reach the age of sixty, they are given a huge party and are greatly honored. After this day, they can wear special clothing, and even strangers will show them respect.

Most Koreans value education. Parents work hard so that their children will have money enough to go to school when public education is finished. They teach their children to respect their teachers and to be loyal to them.

The Korean language is the same all over the peninsula. The style of language changes as a Korean speaks to different people, though. With honored persons, such as teachers or old people, a formal style is used. Strangers are spoken to in the polite style. And the intimate or plain style is used with family members or with children.

We use several different words or expressions to get someone's attention. When we are speaking to an important person, we might say "Pardon me." If we are talking to a friend, we might say "Hello!" In a store, we might get a clerk to notice us by saying "Miss!" or "Sir!" And if we want to get a stranger's attention, we might say "Hey!"

Koreans don't use a different word or expression for all of these situations. They show respect or lack of respect by changing the ending of the verb they are using. For instance, when they wish to be noticed, they can use the same verb, *yobo*, and change the ending of it to address different people:

*Yobosipsio* is the most polite form of address. It is used for honored persons.

*Yoboseyo* is the word commonly used to address both strangers and friends. Koreans use this word when they answer the telephone.

*Yobosio* is used to address someone who waits on you, such as a clerk or waiter.

*Yobo* is used when the speaker has no respect for the listener. It is considered the least polite form of address.

The Korean language is difficult for North Americans to learn because the speaker must change all verb endings when he or she addresses different types of people.

Many of these modern Korean ways may have come from the teachings of an ancient Chinese scholar named Confucius. He lived in the sixth century B.C., and his ideas have been studied in Korea for two thousand years. They have been made Korean.

Confucius tried to think of ways in which people could lead worthy lives. Since his ideas seemed so wise, his words were written down and carried around the world. Many Westerners know Confucian sayings. One is, "Do not do unto others what you would not like yourself."

Confucius made a list of the duties people must think about. Among them was the idea that a person must be loyal—first to parents, second to a leader, third to a husband or wife, fourth to an older brother and younger brother, and fifth to a friend. This idea means that the highest respect must go to one's parents, even after death, when their graves must be tended. In the case of a man and a woman, the man must always be superior.

Education is very important, Confucius said, especially for people in government, who ought to pass many tests to earn their jobs. He felt that people who do their duty lead the most worthy lives.

Many modern Koreans call themselves followers of Confucius. Can you see how his ancient ideas have helped to make their ways?

Another ancient philosopher also helped make modern Korean ways. Siddhartha Gautama, or Buddha, lived in India, and he, too, tried to determine how people could live good lives. His ideas came to Korea in A.D. 372, and over the years they have slowly been changed and made Korean. Many Koreans today, especially women, are Buddhists.

*Many Koreans follow the teachings of Siddhartha Gautama, or Buddha, an Indian philosopher and holy man. His influence on Korea can be seen in the beautiful images* (left) *and the great temples* (above) *that have been made to honor him.*

*Some Buddhist temples in Korea are held to be national treasures. So, too, is the ancient South Gate in the Seoul wall, which is pictured here.*

Buddha taught that people are born again and again until they become perfect. He said that people could find peace and love by giving up worldly pleasures.

Some followers of Buddha in Korea became monks. They built temples far-off in the mountains.

Beautiful paintings were made for these temples, and artists built statues of Buddha for them. Some monks kept written records, and so the temples where they lived became libraries. Other followers of Buddha learned special dances. They played instruments and chanted songs. Beautiful pottery was made to be used in temple services, and bells were cast to call the people to prayer. Buddhist monks and nuns today make sure these objects are protected.

Perhaps because of these ancient beginnings, modern Koreans are very artistic. In Seoul a huge arts and crafts center is the most popular place in the city. Artists from all over the world are invited to come. In P'yŏngyang the people are proud of their giant library center. All over Korea, artists, dancers, writers, and potters are respected.

South Korea has numbered all art of national value. People, places, and things are called treasures. The ancient South Gate in the Seoul wall, mentioned in chapter one, is National Treasure Number 1. Celadon, a special Korean pottery, is world famous. Old pieces of it are national treasures, but new pieces, copied from designs made centuries ago, are sold in many stores.

Modern Koreans value these objects and traditions. Dancers still perform ancient folk dances for special events. In the farmers' dance, men have huge

*Celadon, a special kind of Korean pottery, has become world famous.*

*An ancient Buddhist drum dance features women dressed in decorative costumes.*

streamers on their hats, and they whirl them in the air as they move. Women sometimes dress in traditional clothing and do a Buddhist dance, with drums or cymbals. And many Koreans climb high into the mountains so that they can enjoy the beauty and traditions of their temples.

Other modern ideas come from an even older belief. Koreans feel close to nature. They like walking in forests or hiking over mountains. They like rivers

*Koreans enjoy hiking into the mountains to visit beautiful temples such as this one at Kyŏngju.*

and lakes and parks, and they all want to have growing things nearby. They wonder if there are spirits in nature.

Early Koreans believed that all things in nature have spirits. Like North American Indians, they felt that there was a way to please the spirits of the trees, mountains, caves, animals, and rivers. This ancient belief is called shamanism. The person who could appeal to the unseen spirits was called a shaman.

Long ago shamans were men or women. They had many rules to help people please the unseen spirits all around them. The mountain spirit was especially important. Other important spirits were the turtle, the dragon, the tiger, and the phoenix because people believed that they guarded the whole universe.

Most modern Koreans say that shamanism is just superstition, but they still follow some of the old ideas. Do you ever knock on wood to avoid bad luck? Sometimes people do things just because their ancestors did them. Hundreds of years ago, Koreans built houses with roofs that turned up at the edges. People believed that if evil spirits came down the roof, they would bounce back up again. Today some Korean houses are still built that way, but only because people like the way they look.

There are still shamans—all women—but few

people believe that they can cure illness or chase away evil spirits. Yet some ideas from shamanism still exist. The tiger, the dragon, the turtle, and the phoenix are popular symbols in Korean thought, the dragon being the most powerful symbol. The United Nations military headquarters in the Republic of Korea is called Yong San—Dragon Mountain. There are still shaman dancers in most folk festivals. Korean artwork and writings often center around the mountain spirit, the turtle, the phoenix, the tiger, or the dragon.

Modern Koreans have accepted new religions, too. In 1882 Christian missionaries came to Korea. The newcomers helped the people learn about agriculture and medicine, and they started schools. Many Koreans became Protestants or Catholics.

More than 200 other religions are known in the Republic of Korea, and they all exist peacefully. In the Democratic People's Republic of Korea, old religions have given way to the newer Communist beliefs.

All over Korea, city dwellers seem to accept and use new ideas more easily than the country people do. Perhaps the rural people stay with the old ideas longer because some of them are still living in small villages and don't have much contact with outsiders.

You can see the difference between country and city people in the type of clothing they wear. People in the country are likely to wear the traditional Korean

*People living in rural areas are likely to wear the traditional Korean outfits pictured here.*

costume, especially the men. It is comfortable and cool, light and sensible. The trousers are baggy, tight at the ankle and the waist, and the jacket is loose. The women wear a long, very high-waisted skirt and a short jacket. For formal occasions, the dress will be made of expensive material with designs and bright colors. For everyday wear, it will be plain. Older women will probably continue to dress in the traditional way. Some younger country women are beginning to wear western-style clothing, though.

On busy city streets almost all the people seem to be wearing clothing that is a blend of styles from other countries. In the north, the working people dress very much alike, often wearing high-necked uniforms. In the south, the styles look like fashions seen on any street in an American or Canadian city. Blue jeans are very popular, and they are for sale everywhere. Maybe the jeans you are wearing right now were made in Korea.

The shops in the large cities of the south show how other ideas from the West are blended into Korean ways. On a given street you may find a shoe store offering styles like those worn in Germany, and a clothing store featuring copies of fashions popular in France. There may also be a record shop selling American-type songs, and an artist's shop with English-style paintings. The Koreans make these

*Western styles of dress have become popular in South Korea, especially in the cities.*

things themselves, but they use ideas from other lands. They might use cast-off materials from other lands, too. Metal toys, for example, are sometimes made from American soda cans.

Many shops are just tiny rooms in the private homes of the shopkeepers. You can find almost anything you want in these stores. If you cannot find something, the shopkeeper will tell you that it will be there the next day. "It will be here tomorrow," he or she will smile and say.

When you return the next day, the message will be the same. Koreans do not like to give bad news.

They will rarely show anger either. If Koreans are upset, only a quick intake of breath through clenched teeth will indicate it. They smile or laugh in public, but they do not like to show anger or sadness.

All Koreans work hard. Farmers sometimes plow huge fields with only one ox and a wooden plow. Factories and schools are open many hours six days a week. On the streets and roads, Koreans seem to run rather than walk.

When Hawaiians needed workers for their sugar plantations in 1904, they asked for Koreans. They said that Koreans were the best workers in the world. Today, when other nations need workers for their oil fields or industries, they ask for Korean workers for the same reason.

All of these ways can be understood by remembering Korea's past. When the Koreans were conquered by powerful nations, they had to learn to live with cruel rulers. They had to make good use of the things they owned and find a way to please outsiders while still remaining Korean. As a result, they learned to blend foreign ideas and fashions with those of their own and to use cast-off materials. In addition, they came to value self-control and hard work, and always tried to give good news.

Koreans have been called the most religious, artistic, and hardworking people in the world. Their ways are a blend of old and new ideas, and they are helping modern Koreans build exciting new lives based on fine old traditions.

# 3. The Past Is Always Present

As the people of one of the world's oldest nations, today's Koreans are very proud of their long history. They tell stories about their past and value things which were made many centuries ago. Written records trace their beginnings back to the third century B.C. Legends trace it back much farther than that. Some Koreans tell stories about Tan'gun, who is said to have lived in 2333 B.C.

In the twenty-fourth century B.C., they say, the son of the creator was bored. He told a male tiger and a female bear that he would make them human if they would eat certain plants and live in the dark.

The tiger soon gave up and came back to the sunlight. But the bear remained in the dark for three weeks. When she appeared again, she had turned into a beautiful woman. The son of the creator and this woman became the parents of Tan'gun, the first Korean ruler.

Today, high on a mountain peak on Kanghwa Island, Koreans visit a huge stone altar. Some say it was built by Tan'gun himself. The Seoul government calls this place Treasure Number 136.

The tales about Tan'gun may only be myths, but

another early Korean, Kija, was a real person who lived in 1200 B.C. Records from China tell us that he was unhappy with the rulers there. He and his friends moved south and made their own governments.

Much later, about 200 B.C., many Chinese people began moving farther down into the peninsula. China was building the Great Wall, and many people were forced to become slaves, spending their whole lives working on it. Some of them died, and their bodies were used to help make the wall stronger. Those who could run away tried to escape.

The Chinese who went south met those people who were already settled in Korea. They formed small groups with them, shared ideas, and built villages. As the years passed, people from one group married those of another. In addition, one group joined with another to make war. As a result, the whole peninsula was settled and organized into three kingdoms by the first century A.D.

For the next five centuries, many kings and queens ruled these three kingdoms. Over the years their armies often fought against each other. Finally all three kingdoms came together under a Silla ruler named King Munmu, and most of the peninsula was united. From then on Koreans divide their history into the Silla years, the Koryŏ years, the Yi years, and modern times. The Silla years began in A.D. 668.

(Above) *Huge earthen mounds cover the tombs of many ancient Korean kings.* (Left) *This gold crown was found in one of these tombs.*

Like the rulers before him, King Munmu said that Kyŏngju would be the capital of the country. Tombs for royal people had always been built there, and because of these burial places, today's Koreans know a great deal about their Silla ancestors.

The dead were put in wooden caskets, and treasures were placed all around them. Then a wooden shed was built to cover both the caskets and the treasures. Finally, stones and dirt were piled on top of it to a height of twenty feet, making a huge, sloping hill.

Modern Koreans are still exploring these ancient mounds. In 1921 a crown of pure gold was discovered in a tomb. In 1973 more than 1,000 treasures were found in another one. So far thirty-six royal tombs have been explored, and many of their treasures have been placed in museums.

But King Munmu, first ruler of the united peninsula, did not want to be buried in a tomb with treasures. He said that such things cost too much, and he ordered that his body be thrown into the water when he died. He said his spirit would become a sea dragon and guard the land against attack from Japan. Today you can see an altar that marks King Munmu's watery grave in the sea southeast of Kyŏngju.

The first century of Silla rule was good for the nation because it was peaceful. People were able to travel from one end of the peninsula to another. Ideas about religion, education, and art were shared. Many beautiful Buddhist temples were built.

But the good years of Silla rule soon passed. By A.D. 900 the rulers were too weak to stop the gangs of bandits who were roaming the countryside, killing and robbing. Several military groups then began fighting each other for control of the country.

One group finally became stronger than the Silla government itself. In 935 the last Silla king left, and soon all of the peninsula was under the rule of a general named Wang Kŏn. He renamed the country Koryŏ, from which we get the modern name Korea. The Koryŏ years lasted from 918 to 1392.

Wang Kŏn became the first king of Koryŏ. He was a good ruler, but he worried about strangers taking over his power. He wanted the kingdom to stay with his family, and so he said that brothers and sisters of royalty should become husband and wife.

Today we think that this is very strange. But in the beginning years of the Koryŏ period brothers and sisters often married each other, keeping the government's power in one family. Since this brought peace, good things began happening all over the peninsula again. Artists made beautiful celadon pottery and painted beautiful pictures. Poetry was written, more temples were built, and new schools were opened.

As the years passed, the country's rulers once again grew weak. Then armies of Mongols, fierce tribes from central Asia, invaded the land. In 1232 the Koryŏ king fled to Kanghwa Island, leaving his people to be killed and their lands to be burned.

The Mongols destroyed many of the good things

the Koreans had created. Among them were thousands of wooden blocks that Buddhist monks had carefully carved to print the words of Buddha. Since 80,000 blocks needed to be carved, this task had taken a very long time. Yet it was finished long before people in the Western world had thought about making a printing press.

By 1251 the Buddhist monks had finished the task again. This time the blocks were saved from the invading armies. Today you can see them—they are called Treasure Number 32—in a temple in the Kaya Mountains. The Koreans are glad that some of their valuable treasures were protected during those long ago, terrible years.

After conquering most of Korea, the Mongols forced the Koryŏ kings to marry Mongol women, and they took control of the government. Under the Mongols' rule, people began starving because their homes and farms were destroyed. Korean men were forced to join the Mongol army because the conquerors now wished to invade Japan, too.

The Japanese chased the invaders from their land. Then small groups of Japanese pirates began attacking the Korean peninsula from the sea. The Korean people suffered terrible hardships, but their Mongol kings didn't care.

King Kongyang was the last ruler during the

Koryŏ years. Some say he was the cruelest king of all. As his people starved, his hunting parties trampled crops growing in the fields.

Yi Sŏng-gye was his best Korean general. General Yi loved his country, and he tried to obey his king. But when King Kongyang wanted to invade Manchuria, General Yi said it was madness. Still, he felt he had to follow the king's orders. Stories say that he wept as he led his troops north because he knew they would not return.

But General Yi did not cross the Yalu River in the north. Instead, he returned to the south with his army and took over the Koryŏ government. Seoul became the new capital, and the Mongols were gradually chased from the country. Those who did remain adopted new ideas and became Koreans.

General Yi became the new king of the peninsula in 1392, one hundred years before Columbus discovered America. The government he began ruled Korea until 1910.

During the centuries of the Yi rulers, Japan often invaded the peninsula. Koreans began talking about being a small shrimp in the sea between two powerful whales, China and Japan. Whenever there was war, the Koreans were starved and killed because their nation was never as strong as the others.

But many good things happened during those

years, too. Two of Korea's greatest heroes—one a king and the other a sailor—lived then.

King Sejong, now called "Sejong the Great," ruled from 1419 to 1450. He did many wise and wonderful things for his country. One of his greatest achievements was to invent a Korean way of writing.

Until Sejong's time, the Koreans had always used the Chinese way of writing, even though their language was different. Chinese writing is very difficult. It tries to show the meaning of a word rather than the sound. Its symbols, called characters, are like small pictures, and sometimes a writer must use twenty-five lines to form just one of them. To read or write Chinese, an educated person should know at least 20,000 characters.

King Sejong said that the Koreans needed their own form of writing, one which used the sound of words. He and his wise men made a beautiful but simple alphabet which they called *Han'gŭl*.

"A wise person can learn Han'gŭl in a few hours," said King Sejong. "Even a foolish person can learn it in ten days."

He wanted everyone to accept the new alphabet, and so he tried to think of ways to impress his people. One story tells us that he had the symbols written in honey on leaves. The next day, when important vis-

*King Sejong was one of Korea's most important rulers. He and his wise men invented Han' gŭl, the Korean alphabet.*

itors walked in his garden, they thought that the letters had been carved in the leaves by a god. They did not suspect that insects had chewed out the shapes of the letters while eating the honey and said that the new alphabet had been sent from heaven.

Today people all over the world say this alphabet is the finest one ever invented. It has twenty-four symbols, and each symbol is useful as well as beautiful. (See p. 137 for a list of these symbols.) Han'gŭl has helped Koreans become one of the best educated peoples in the world. Today they honor King Sejong and his alphabet with a special holiday every October 9.

Admiral Yi Sun-sin, the sailor, is honored because he stopped an invasion in 1592. The Japanese had entered Korea through Pusan, a seaport on the east coast, and they were winning every battle. If Admiral Yi had not driven off their ships, they probably would have conquered the country.

The admiral ordered iron plates to be made for his ships. He also commanded that they be fitted with an iron ram in the shape of a turtle's head. Then he sailed out to fight the Japanese.

The Japanese sailors were surprised to find that the iron-plated ships would not burn. Some sailors thought the ships were devils from another world, and they backed away. Admiral Yi still managed to

(Left) *Admiral Yi Sun-sin was one of Korea's greatest war heroes. In 1592 he used iron-plated "turtle ships"* (above) *to drive away some Japanese invaders.*

set a number of Japanese ships on fire, however, and many of them sank.

The success of Admiral Yi's "turtle ships" inspired the Koreans. Spurred on by his victories, they drove the Japanese from their country. Today he is honored as one of Korea's greatest war heroes.

A woman who resisted the Japanese in 1592 is honored today, too. Non'gae was a dancing girl who lived near the coastal city of Chinju. The Japanese won a big victory there, and they celebrated by forcing some Korean women to dance for them near a cliff by the sea. Instead of dancing, Non'gae threw herself at the Japanese general, and they both fell over the cliff.

When her friends saw what she had done, they threw themselves at the Japanese soldiers, too. Many of the soldiers fell over the cliff and were killed. Today the Koreans honor Non'gae's memory on a large stone called the Rock of Faithful Women. On it they have written, "Eternally as the river may the memory of her loyalty live!"

The Yi rulers had to fight more wars in the years after Admiral Yi's victory. Manchu troops from China invaded the peninsula in the seventeenth century, and once again the people were starved and killed. Finally, the Yi leaders agreed to pay the Manchus a huge sum of money and the fighting stopped.

After invasions by the Mongols, the Japanese, and the Manchus, the Koreans wanted to be left alone. They closed their country to all foreigners and became the Hermit Kingdom.

But new ideas were moving into their country whether they wanted them or not. In the eighteenth century, Catholic missionaries tried to preach in Korea. Some were killed, but more came. Western ideas were reaching everywhere.

By the end of the nineteenth century, the Yi kings were losing power. Kojong, the last of the Yi rulers, was only twelve years old when he was crowned king. Scheming adults around him really ran the country. They listened to the ideas of the Japanese, who were trying to get power again, and killed anyone who disagreed with them.

In 1876 the Japanese forced the Koreans to open some of their ports to trade. Then after winning victories over China and Russia, they slowly took over the country. King Kojong and Queen Minn lost their power as well as their army. Finally, the country was officially declared to be part of Japan in 1910, and Japanese officials took control of the government.

Koreans today say that under this Japanese rule, their country suffered more than it ever had before. They were glad when Japan lost World War II and left Korea.

Their happiness turned to sadness when they saw what happened in 1945. The Soviet Union and the United States each took power, dividing the whole country in half. The north became the Democratic People's Republic of Korea, under Communist rule, and the south became the Republic of Korea, guided first by the United States and later by the United Nations.

In 1950 the Korean War broke out, with people

from the north fighting people from the south. Once again, the Koreans said, powerful nations were destroying their land. Once again cities were ruined and people starved.

The fighting ended in 1953, but the peninsula remains divided, and soldiers from many nations are still stationed there. In addition, some families are still separated, and no one can freely cross the demilitarized, or cease-fire, zone between the two countries.

Yet the cities have been rebuilt, and most people are no longer poor or hungry. The two Koreas are each becoming leaders in modern industry, and many good things are happening in both countries.

Kim Il Sung has been president of the Democratic People's Republic since its beginning, and many there think of him as a glorious leader. Under his rule, all businesses belong to the government, and few things are privately owned. In addition, the people must follow Communist beliefs instead of religious ones.

Some Koreans say that because the government tells people what to do, they are able to have the best kind of life. They are all comrades working for the same cause. Others are unhappy because they want more freedom of choice. They wish they could have their own farms and businesses, and follow their own religious beliefs, but they are afraid to protest.

The government in South Korea has had several leaders. There have been riots against some of them because many people felt that the government was unfair. Syngman Rhee (who wrote his name in the Western way, with the family name last) was the first president. Many modern Koreans say that he was a terrible dictator. (A dictator is a person who holds complete power in a country.) Another president, Park Chung Hee, was assassinated, or killed, in 1979. In 1981 Chun Doo Hwan took office as the twelfth president of the Republic of Korea.

Many Koreans believe that this government is better than the one in the north because the people have more freedom. Under it more than one person can run for president. People can have their own farms or businesses and choose their own religions. There has been trouble in the past, some say, because when people are free to choose, they may have disagreements. South Koreans tell each other that they are glad they don't live in the north, where people are not free to protest or make changes.

Because of the differences between the governments in the north and the south, the two Koreas are bitter enemies. Many people fear that a war might even break out between them. Their fears were heightened in October 1983 when seventeen South Koreans were killed in a bombing attack in Rangoon,

Burma. The Burmese police stated that North Korean terrorists were probably responsible for this attack.

Most South Koreans were outraged by this news. Some of them wanted to take immediate action against the North Koreans, but their leaders decided to respond with words instead of bullets. Nevertheless, ill-feeling between the two countries remains very high.

North Korea's close ties to the Soviet Union have made the situation worse. Most South Koreans have long considered the Soviets their enemies and want to have no dealings with them. Some have even gone so far as to call the Soviets barbarians for shooting down a South Korean airliner that accidentally crossed into Soviet territory in September 1983. All 269 people on board the weaponless plane were killed.

In spite of these tragic events, Koreans in both the south and the north believe that better days will come. They hope that, in time, their country will be united once again and that it will be open and free for all Koreans.

# 4. *What the People Say*

Have you ever heard anyone remark, "That's like finding a needle in a haystack"? It's an old saying we use to show that something is almost impossible. Who, after all, could ever find a tiny needle in a huge haystack?

The Koreans have a saying to show that something is almost impossible, too. They say, "That's like going to Seoul to find Mr. Kim." If a person knew only the name Mr. Kim, he could never find the right man in Seoul. There are hundreds of thousands of Mr. Kims in Korea, and many of them live in this city.

Old sayings, or proverbs, tell a lot about a country and its people. Since all humans are very much alike, some sayings are the same in every country. Others are different because each country's history is different.

Over the centuries the Koreans have often not had enough food to eat, and so many of their sayings are about food. In the past, when two Koreans met, they frequently greeted each other with a polite question: "Have you eaten your honorable food, sir?" And they told each other that they hoped the Spirit of Hunger would not fly inside of their house gates.

Often, too, Korean people have not had enough money to buy expensive clothing. For this reason they have an old saying that states, "If it is the same price, then buy the crimson skirt." They mean that everyone likes bright colors, but colored clothing is more expensive. Hats have also been prized because of their cost. Koreans say, "Wear a hat to meet disgrace," because a man with a fine hat can feel some pride even in failure.

Because few of us have ever had to go without food or clothing during war, we don't have many sayings about these things. But some of our other sayings are very much like those of the Koreans. The words may be different, but the meanings are the same. Let's look at some examples.

When Koreans begin a make-believe story, they say, "When tigers smoked long pipes..." We might say, "Once upon a time..." We both mean that the story we're about to tell never really happened. Likewise, Koreans say, "If lightning flashes, there will be a clap of thunder," while we say, "Where there's smoke, there's fire." We both mean that signs and events go together.

The Koreans also say, "It takes the clap of two hands to make a sound." We might say, "It takes two to quarrel." Yet we both mean that two people are needed to do some things. Similarly, Koreans say,

"Too many kitchen monks break the cooking kettle," while we say, "Too many cooks spoil the broth." Both of us mean that sometimes it is better if only one person does a task.

Like many of us, the Koreans believe it's wise to enjoy the present because nobody knows what the future will bring. They say, "A bar of candy today is sweeter than a bowl of honey tomorrow." We say, "A bird in the hand is worth two in the bush," or "Don't count your chickens before they are hatched."

Each of these old sayings tells us about a nation's people. So do old folktales, stories which are passed down from one generation to the next. By hearing them, we can tell what kinds of people or animals have been admired and what kinds have been thought foolish. In Korea there are many folktales about animals.

In some stories, the tiger, or Mountain King, appears in order to warn good people about evil things. He often pretends to be an old man, as he did with Yongpalee, a Korean man who was resting in the mountains. The old man gave Yongpalee a magic eyelash. Using it, Yongpalee could look at people and see whether they were good or evil.

Dragons rewarded good people in these folktales, too. They were thought to have great power, and one of them was said to rule the bottom of the sea. One tale tells how this Dragon King saved a girl, Sim Chung, because she was such a good daughter.

Sim Bang Sa, her father, needed three hundred bags of rice in order to be cured of his blindness. But he was very poor, and so he thought that his situation was hopeless. He knew that he and his daughter could never get so many bags of rice.

Then Sim Chung heard that a shipload of sailors was willing to pay a great price for a young woman. They wanted to toss her into the ocean if the waves became rough during their voyage. She would be a gift for the Dragon King, they said, and then he would make the sea calm again.

Sim Chung made a bargain with the sailors. They brought the rice to her father, and she went on their ship.

Soon after they sailed away, a terrible storm came up. "Help! Help!" screamed the sailors. "The monstrous dragon is coming! Help!" Quickly they threw Sim Chung into the angry waves.

Because she had been willing to die for her father's sake, the Dragon King took pity on her. He sent her back to shore in a wave of lotus blossoms. When her blind old father heard her voice again, he was so overjoyed that he cried, and his happy tears cured his blindness.

These folktales about dragons and tigers are not

true, of course, but the Koreans have always felt that these animals are special. In the past, they pasted pictures of a dragon and a tiger on the doors of their houses so that the strength of these animals would chase away evil spirits. Likewise, the middle beam of the roof usually had the Chinese characters for dragon and tiger written on it. And when someone died, Koreans said that the person had ridden the dragon to the distant shore.

Modern Koreans still admire dragons and tigers. They like to build their homes facing south, with mountains on the east and the west. The mountain on the east side is called the Blue Dragon, and the one on the west is called the White Tiger. This arrangement means that the family will have good fortune. Small children are called "little dragon" as a mark of affection, and *yong*, the Korean word for dragon, is still part of the name of many Korean males because it suggests the idea of strength.

Other kinds of animals have been popular in Korean folktales for different reasons. Often the people liked to tell funny stories about small, clever animals who were able to get the best of those who were big and powerful. One of Korea's favorite folktales shows how a rabbit's brain won out over even the power of the Dragon King.

When tigers smoked long pipes, the Dragon King

had a terrible stomachache. All the animals at the bottom of the sea worried about him. Finally one of the doctors had an idea. "You need to eat the liver of a rabbit," he said.

"I'll go to shore and bring back a rabbit," a huge turtle said. "I'll bring him back alive so the liver will be fresh. Once he is here, the doctors can cut him up so the Dragon King can eat his liver."

The turtle swam powerful strokes until he reached the shore. As he climbed out on to the land, he saw a small rabbit. "Come jump on my back," he called. "I'll take you for a ride across the water and show you the Dragon King's palace."

The rabbit thought that was a fine idea, and so he rode through the waves, proudly standing on the back of the turtle. When they finally reached the palace, the Dragon King shouted, "Now I can eat the liver of this rabbbit!"

The rabbit was frightened but clever. "What?" he cried. "No one told me to bring my liver along! I left it at home in a secret place in the mountain. If I had known that the great Dragon King had need of it, I would certainly have brought it!"

"Take this rabbit back to shore!" the Dragon King commanded the turtle, "so that he can get his liver for me!" And so the turtle gave the rabbit another ride back through the waves.

As soon as his feet were on dry land, the rabbit hopped away from the turtle. "Thank you for the ride home!" he shouted, laughing. "And you can be sure that neither you nor the Dragon King will ever see me or my liver again!" Then, still laughing, he ran off into the forest.

In another story, the rabbit outwits a tiger. This tiger had fallen into a deep pit, and he cried so loudly that an old woodcutter finally leaned down and helped him out. As soon as he was free, he began to roar. "You were foolish enough to let me out—now I'm going to eat you!"

"But I was clever!" said the woodcutter. "Didn't I get you out of that terrible pit? You ought to be grateful to me."

They made such a racket arguing back and forth that a rabbit heard them and stopped to listen. "I can solve this problem," he told them. "I can tell which one of you is wise and which one is foolish. But I must hear the whole story."

"Good," said the tiger. "We'll tell you everything. You can be the judge."

The rabbit came closer. "Now then, I must understand this from the very beginning. What happened first?"

"I was down there in that deep pit," the tiger said.

"I must see," said the rabbit. "If I am to judge, I

must see it all. Just where were you standing down in that pit?"

The tiger jumped into the deep hole. "I was right here," he called up, "and then he—"

"And then *we* both left," the rabbit told him, laughing. And he and the happy woodcutter hurried off, while the tiger roared from the bottom of the pit.

Many Korean folktales deal with unseen spirits who enter into humans or animals. These stories reflect the early Koreans' belief in shamanism, which you learned about in chapter two.

One story tells about a frog prince. It says that a Prince of the Stars was sent down from the sky to live his life as a frog because he had made his father angry. When a beautiful young woman was willing to marry him, he turned back into the handsome son of the Star King. Then he and his bride became two new stars shining in the sky.

Sometimes enchanted animals speak to humans, as did a deer to a kind woodcutter. The deer told him how to win the love of a Princess of Heaven. By his cleverness, he won her love, and they both became living stars in the Milky Way.

Birds, too, may be enchanted. In a tale about two brothers, one good and one evil, a sparrow gives a magic seed to the good brother, who has helped him after the evil brother has refused. When the seed sprouts, it has huge pods filled with gold, silver, silk, and jewels.

"What a grand reward for simply helping a wounded sparrow," the evil brother says when he sees all the riches. He decides that he wants a reward, too. And so he finds a sparrow in the forest and throws rocks at it until its legs are broken.

"Help me!" the sparrow cries.

"Only if you give me a magic seed!" the evil brother answers.

The sparrow promises, and so the brother helps him. When the bird's legs are healed, he gives the evil brother a seed and flies away.

"Now I will be wealthy, too!" the man says. His seed finally sprouts, and it produces large pods. But when the pods open, only frogs, toads, snakes, and demons jump out, and they immediately begin to beat him.

Maybe some of the ideas from these old Korean tales seem familiar to you. Many of our own stories have the same thoughts in them. People all over the world like to hear that wisdom and strength are valuable, that goodness ought to be rewarded, and that evil should be punished. Most folktales show that all living creatures are tied together in some way, and that much in life is a mystery.

You can make up stories that have these same

ideas. But if you want to sound like a real Korean, start your tale with the words, "When tigers smoked long pipes..."

# 5. Holidays, Holidays

Since Korea is a land where old traditions blend in with new ideas, the people use two kinds of calendars. The ancient one, adopted from the Chinese, is based on the cycle of the moon. This lunar, or moon-based, calendar may have as many as thirteen months. The months have no special names but are simply numbered. The newer solar, or sun-based, calendar, adopted from the West, is exactly like the one you know. It has twelve months and 365 days.

Koreans use both of these calendars to determine the date of the yearly events they celebrate. Traditional celebrations are dated according to the lunar calendar, more modern ones according to the solar calendar. Because of the two kinds of calendars, the people have two sets of holidays to celebrate each year.

New Year's Day, the biggest holiday, is observed on both calendars. Rural areas still use the lunar calendar, according to which the celebration starts on the first day of the first moon in a new year. Since the appearance of a new moon varies from year to year, the actual date might fall sometime in February according to the solar calendar. Most city people, however, celebrate New Year's Day on January 1, just as you do.

No matter when or where the holiday is celebrated in Korea, many customs are the same. People put on their best clothing, take time off from work, and gather together with their families. New Year's Day is a time for children to show respect to their elders and for all family members to honor their ancestors.

Ancient Koreans, who believed in good and evil spirits, thought that people had to stay awake all night on the last night of a year in order to keep bad fortune away in the future. Children were sometimes told that their eyebrows would turn white if they fell asleep before the night was over.

Today few people believe these old ideas, but just for fun a few older brothers and sisters may put white wheat flour on the eyebrows of little ones who are still sleeping. This helps to make New Year's Day a time for joy and laughter as well as solemn ceremony.

Bowing politely to older family members on this day is a ceremony most children enjoy. In some villages, they must seek out each adult male in all the houses and bow to him before fifteen days have passed. In return they are given small gifts, roasted chestnuts, dried persimmons, honey candy, or a few coins.

*Korean children begin the New Year's Day celebration by bowing politely to older family members.*

In all households, children bow to their parents and grandparents as the day begins. Food, drink, guests, gifts, and games are all part of the celebration. Most families feast together, and many have a special New Year's soup made from beef broth, seaweed, and rice. There may be rice cakes and pine nuts with honey for dessert. After the meal, the adults often visit inside while the children go outside to play.

Long ago, Koreans celebrated the arrival of a new year for fifteen days. Boys made special kites and set them free on the fifteenth day. The kites were supposed to carry off all evil spirits as they flew away. Today boys don't believe in evil spirits, but they still make or buy kites and fly them if they can. Before they set their kites loose, some boys attach a paper to them which says, "Away Evils, Come Blessings."

The girls may do other things outside if the weather is good enough. One of their favorite activities is jumping on low seesaws. These boards are balanced low to the ground, and when a girl bounces on one end, the girl at the other end is sent high up into the air. This custom started centuries ago when girls over the age of eight could not leave their courtyards. By bouncing on seesaws, the girls could look over the high courtyard and see the world outside.

After a day of visiting, feasting, and game playing, Koreans may end their celebrations by singing. Many parties conclude with each guest singing a short solo. Some people say that songs and music are Korea's greatest treasure.

Few modern Koreans celebrate the new year for fifteen days, but some children still remember the customs of their ancestors on the fifteenth day. In the past, this was people's last chance to try to make certain that they would have good fortune in the

*If the weather is good enough for playing outside on New Year's Day, Korean girls enjoy jumping on low seesaws.*

coming year, and they looked hard for good luck charms. The number nine was considered especially lucky. Today some children still try to do something nine times to have good luck. For example, they may wash their faces or brush their hair nine times. But anything they do is just for fun.

In the spring, another favorite holiday appears on the lunar calendar in the south—Buddha's birthday. It is celebrated on the eighth day of the fourth month. Since many Koreans are Buddhists, there are many religious activities on this day.

Thousands of people dress in their best clothing and walk to Buddhist temples so that they can offer gifts and special prayers to their ancestors—the Honored Dead. The shaven-headed monks decorate the temples with brightly colored papers and musical chimes or mobiles. They wear their best robes for the occasion.

People remove their shoes at the entrance to the temples. They quietly offer gifts to Buddha—rice cakes, candy, nuts. The monks may pour green tea over a statue of the infant Buddha as a special offering. They may also burn incense, a material that gives off a pleasant smell. Their quiet chanting can often be heard in the smaller huts which surround many main temples.

When the day ends, brightly colored lanterns are

brought out, and the candles inside them are lighted. Their light is supposed to remind people of Buddha's love. It also links people with their ancestors from more than two thousand years ago, who also brought offerings and prayers to Buddha.

The next big lunar holiday is strictly for fun. On the fifth day of the fifth month, Koreans celebrate *Tano*, or "Swing Day." It occurs when the first harvest from the land is ready, and so the weather is usually good.

Most Tano activities are held outside. In rural areas, whole villages gather for outdoor events, while in the cities, people flock to parks and cultural centers, where children have free entertainment. Wrestling, dancing, swinging, and puppet shows are popular in many areas. Women and girls especially enjoy swinging, and villages may erect a swing support that is over twenty feet high. Men take part in various events. A bull may be given to the man who wins the wrestling matches that are held throughout the day.

The last big lunar holiday is *Ch'usŏk*, or "Harvest Moon." Ch'usŏk is much like our Thanksgiving, and it combines the best parts of other holidays. Since it comes on the day of the full moon in the eighth month, it is always celebrated in the fall, when the hardest part of harvesting is over. People are glad to rest and relax. They pause to pay respect to the mem-

*Women and girls often celebrate Tano by riding on swings whose supports are sometimes over twenty feet high.*

ory of their ancestors and to give thanks for the blessings of families.

Like most of us, the Koreans think holidays should center around food, friends, and family. For Ch'usŏk they gather together for a feast, and they visit with their relatives. Later in the day, when the moon is bright in the sky, there may be outside activities. In the villages, the people may dance and sing far into the night. In the cities, the parks will be crowded.

But the real meaning of the day is expressed in the

ceremonies people hold with their own families. In some homes, the men will gather at midnight to read the names of the Honored Dead. Some people say that the spirits of their ancestors are close at this time.

There are other lunar holidays, too, but New Year's Day, Buddha's birthday, Tano, and Ch'usŏk are the favorites of the children.

There are also many solar holidays, but most of them seem to be most interesting for adults, since they concern political matters. The north and the south each celebrate national days, when soldiers march in huge parades and the machines of war are displayed. The children usually enjoy the parades and air shows, but they are not much interested in all the long speeches that follow. They prefer the solar holidays especially planned for children.

April 5, Arbor Day, is a very important holiday. In the Republic of Korea, schoolchildren are given the day off in order to plant trees on the mountainsides.

Children like Han'gŭl Day, too. Every October 9, Koreans honor King Sejong for inventing their fine alphabet, and the people make trips to parks and forests. Some travel by bus to visit Yong-nun, the tomb of King Sejong, where special activities take place. In October the weather is usually good, and so many families go out on hikes and picnics.

December 25 is another grand holiday in the south. When Christianity was brought to Korea, some Koreans started celebrating this day in much the same way that we do. Today Korean Christians have artificial Christmas trees, and they exchange presents and attend church. They sing Christmas carols and gather with their families exactly the way we do. In Seoul, many department stores are decorated with bright lights and colorful ornaments.

Besides these national holidays every Korean can celebrate two other special days just for himself or herself. One occurs when a child has his or her first birthday, for on this day the child formally enters society. Korean babies are considered one year old at birth, and so at the first birthday party they are said to be two years old. If you and a Korean child had been born on the very same day, the Korean would be a whole year older than you!

The women of the house prepare a special seaweed soup for invited guests on this special day. They also dress the birthday child in the finest clothing. Then after relatives and guests arrive, a small table is placed in front of the child, and many items are put on top of it. The adults enjoy guessing which item the child might take first. If he picks yarn, for instance, people say he will have long life. If she picks money, they say she will be blessed with wealth. After this

*Korean children receive a great many presents on their first birthday. Adults enjoy guessing which gift the boy or girl will pick up first.*

ceremony, gifts are presented, and later the family and guests enjoy food and visiting.

The second big celebration for each person occurs on his or her sixtieth birthday. This special day is called *Hwan'gap*, and it usually inspires the finest party the family can afford. All the sons, daughters, and grandchildren come to pay respects.

In Korea respect can be shown by the type of bow one uses. At a Hwan'gap celebration, the bows are deep, with men putting their knees and hands flat on the floor, their foreheads touching their hands. The girls and women make deep, graceful movements, too. After this formal ceremony, friends and relatives feast on a great variety of foods with the honored person.

Long ago, when this celebration was rare because few people lived so long, families spent far more than they could afford for these parties. Today the parties are more private and less expensive, but they are still observed with respect and hold deep meaning.

Like the national holidays based on the solar and the lunar calendars, these two celebrations show that Koreans enjoy being with family members for their special days. Holidays are family days all over the world.

# 6. *There's No Place Like* Chip

Just as you think your home and family are important, Koreans think that their homes and families are special, too. Seeing or hearing the Korean word for the family home—*chip*—nearly always suggests good thoughts to them.

Korean houses have slowly changed over the centuries. Long ago huts were made of mud or clay, and they had thatched roofs and vine-covered walls. Today they are made of wood and concrete and have tiled roofs. In the past, Korean parents and their adult sons lived next to each other. Their houses were arranged so as to form a large hollow square, with a courtyard and a garden in the middle. One man and his sons built the houses for the whole family.

Many people are usually needed to build modern Korean homes, and all the members of one family can rarely live close together. In crowded cities there are huge apartment buildings. Gardens, so important in the past, are still loved, but today's family might have only a few plants on a balcony or a shrub on a skyscraper rooftop. Because of the times, some ideas about housing have changed.

Other features of Korean homes are just the same

now as they were centuries ago. In the past, single-family homes had roofs with upturned edges; new single-family dwellings today might have them, too. Likewise, Koreans have never felt the need of large, spacious rooms in their homes. A family of six or seven might be very happy living in three small rooms. They would use special screens to block off sections for different activities. Not many Koreans can imagine living in a two or three bedroom home.

There are some homes in both the country and the city that do not have electricity or running water, but country homes are especially likely not to be very modern. Many homes in far-off villages have neither television nor household machines.

If there is no running water in a city home, family members can use a public bathhouse, where a small fee will buy soap and towels. Rural people must often share the use of a common well and bathe in nearby lakes or rivers. Water for cooking and cleaning must be carried home. Family members make sure that there is enough water for everyone. They like their homes and clothing to be clean.

In both the country and the city, men carry huge loads by using a *chiggehs*, a large wooden backpack. Westerners call it an A-frame because it looks like the letter *A*. Women sometimes carry a bucket of water on their head and a baby on their back.

*This woodcarving shows the A-frame backpack that Korean men use to carry heavy loads.*

Because of their different working hours, people in the city and the country have different daily schedules. City people can generally count on spending a fixed number of hours at work and at home. Country people, who are mainly farmers, must plan their days according to the weather. If it is good, they will put in many hours working in their fields. If it is bad, they will spend time at home.

No matter where Koreans live, respect and politeness are important in every family. The grandparents, *haraboji* ("grandfather") and *halmŏni* ("grandmother"), may or may not be in the same house, but wherever they live, they will be visited and respected. The father, *aboji*, is honored and obeyed. In the past, *ŏmŏni*, the mother, always stayed at home, but today she may have a job outside of it.

Some Korean men still think that all women belong at home with the children, but others have changed their minds about women working. For centuries most Korean children thought of ŏmŏni as the kind parent and aboji as the stern one, but these roles are changing, too. All over the peninsula men and women are beginning to work together more, although the old idea that sons are more important than daughters is still held.

One ancient idea is modern now. Since A.D. 500, outsiders have liked the way Koreans heat their houses. Today, in our energy-conscious world, their heating method is being copied in many other countries. By using a system of channels stretching under the floors, Koreans have long used the heat from their kitchen cooking fires to warm their homes.

In the past, when sons returned to the family home with their brides, many people used a common kitchen hearth. Heat from the steady fires cooking all the food was carried along in pipes under the floors in several directions, providing a cheap and simple way to warm other areas in the house. This form of heating, known as *ondol*, was used in every household.

Although some Koreans now have gas or electric furnaces, ondol heating is still widely used. A central heating source has channels which lead out to nearby homes. The government in Seoul praises this method because it saves energy. In P'yŏngyang and other cities of the north, huge power stations send heat through hot water pipes stretching under the floors of many houses. With heat rising from these special floors, a house feels warm and comfortable during long winter months.

Perhaps because of this special heating method, Korean families have many activities which take place next to the warm floors. Until modern times, chairs were never used at all. Family members squatted or sat on mats or pillows.

Beds, too, were rarely used. All Koreans in the past, and many yet today, simply rolled out special bedding at night, placed it on the warm floor, and slept on it. The next day, they aired the bedding out, rolled it up, and then put it away. You might like sleeping this way. You would be warm and comfortable all night, and in the morning, there would be no bed to make.

Long ago, no rooms in Korean houses were used just for sleeping. Today some Koreans have bedrooms in their homes, but most of them—especially those in crowded cities—cannot afford to have rooms which are used only for sleeping. Living rooms are used for dining rooms and sleeping quarters.

At some time in the past, Koreans decided that shoes worn outside a house should not be worn inside it. This custom is still observed today in Korean homes. All family members and all polite guests remove their shoes at the door and put on special slippers or stay in their stocking feet when they come inside. As in the past, the floors of a Korean home are expected to be clean and clear, polished and neat.

Long ago, eating always took place near the floors. Low tables, much like beautiful wooden trays with legs, were placed so that each family member could sit on the floor and eat alone. Male members of the household were always served first, and talking

*Some Koreans eat their meals while seated on the floor, using the kind of low table pictured here.*

while eating was considered rude. Only chopsticks and spoons were used, and people ate without smiling or talking.

Today many of these customs have changed. Some Korean homes have tables and chairs exactly like those that you use, and the whole family eats together. Many Koreans are familiar with knives and forks, but usually only chopsticks and spoons are used at home. Even very small children use chopsticks. Koreans feel that learning to use the long slender tools helps develop the children's minds. If you have ever tried using chopsticks, you know how much skill it takes.

The Koreans love to have guests come to their homes, and they often spend more than they can afford in order to entertain them. Guests are honored persons, and they get the finest foods. They always begin eating first, and if they like a certain food, the hostess will make sure that more of that dish is carried to the table.

If you are invited to eat in a Korean home, you should be sure that you do not take the last of anything. According to custom, there must always be more of everything on the tables, in case the guest should want it. Be sure that you don't click your soup spoon against your teeth as you eat, for this shows bad manners. Sometimes a host will offer plain rice as the last thing served. It would be an insult to accept it, though. If you are still hungry enough to eat plain rice after all the special foods are served, then the host and hostess will worry that they did not have enough to please you.

The food served in a Korean home centers around rice, which is served three times a day. You might think rice for breakfast is unusual, but a Korean your age would think that cold cereal is stranger still. Rice can be fixed in so many ways that it is always tasty. Workers and schoolchildren carry it in special containers so that they can eat it at lunchtime, too.

*Kimch'i* is another staple, or basic food, in the

Koreans' diet. There are at least nine different ways to prepare this vegetable dish. In the past, kimch'i was popular because it could be served all winter long. The people were able to preserve it in earthenware jars, and they could eat it all through the cold months, when its vitamins and minerals were needed. Today, even though many Koreans have refrigerators, kimch'i is popular simply because it tastes so good.

Korean women have "kimch'i days" every fall, when Chinese cabbages, turnips, radishes, cucumbers, and red peppers are on sale in large outdoor marketplaces. At least one hundred and seventy-five large heads of cabbage must be purchased to supply a mother, father, and three children with kimch'i all winter. The kimch'i is stored in jars so large that you would be able to hide inside one. These jars may be kept outside on a balcony or placed in a yard near a house. Some people bury their jars in the ground because extreme temperature can spoil the kimch'i.

The women work very hard washing, cutting, and preparing the vegetables. Hot red peppers are dried in the sun for several days. The cabbage is soaked in salt brine. Slowly, more things are added. Some kinds of kimch'i have chestnuts, pears, or apples; others have octopus, squid, or shrimp. Peppers, garlic, and leeks make some kinds very hot and spicy, but other kinds are milder tasting.

*Kimch'i jars come in a variety of sizes. Some are so big that a child could fit inside them.*

In the spring, cucumber kimch'i is made from fresh cucumbers. It is not expected to last long, so it is not preserved in salt or other spices. Often a special stuffing is placed inside whole cucumbers, and they are all eaten within two or three days.

Soybean dishes are also common. Korean cooks make sauce, cakes, flour, and casseroles with this important vegetable. Sprouts can be grown from soybeans, too, for use in soups or salads. All types of meat are used with soybeans, but fish is the most common, since others, especially beef, are very expensive. In the past, snake meat, dog meat, and insects were eaten with soybean dishes, but today these items are not seen very often.

Many fruits and vegetables are similar to the ones you eat, but others are special. Fresh red persimmons are especially popular. This red fruit looks much like a tomato, but it grows on a tree, and its pulp is yellow and sweet. Children can hardly wait until persimmons ripen in the fall.

Another popular fruit looks like a large, round yellow apple, but it doesn't taste like one. It has a sweet, juicy flavor much like very ripe pears. Many kinds of melons and berries from all over the peninsula are available during the warm months. In wintertime, fruits are sent up from Cheju Island. Cheju tangerines are always good.

*These villagers are stringing persimmons on ropes woven from grass. The fruit will then be hung up to dry.*

You may already have eaten a very popular Korean dish—*ramyon*, a noodle with special flavoring. In Korea it is made fresh, but it is also dried and packaged as an instant food for sale in other countries. You can find ramyon in almost any grocery store and fix it yourself, since it can easily be prepared with boiling water.

The secret of good Korean home cooking is in the long, careful preparation of the food. Washing, cutting, and chopping the food usually takes longer than cooking it. Seasoning and spices are very important, too. Korean cooks use a lot of garlic and sesame seeds.

You and your family might like to try some Korean dishes. Listed below are four recipes that can be fixed in your home.

### *Rice Omelet*

3 cups cooked white rice
1/2 pound beef (or ground beef)
1/2 carrot, diced
1/2 onion, diced
3 tablespoons tomato ketchup
1/2 teaspoon salt
1/2 teaspoon pepper
3 eggs
3 tablespoons salad oil

Dice beef, carrot, and onion. Cook beef in frying pan with salad oil until brown. Add carrot and onion. When mixture is cooked, add tomato ketchup and cooked rice. Sprinkle with salt and pepper, and mix thoroughly. Remove from heat. Make individual omelet in crepe shape using one egg. Place mixed rice in the middle and wrap it with egg. Omelet may be served with a pickle.

## Fried Egg Roll

1 pound ground beef
1 pound bean cake (tofu)
1 pound bean sprouts (may use canned bean
  sprouts)
1 egg
1 package egg roll skins
2/3 cup oil
Mixture A:
    2 tablespoons chopped green onion
    1 teaspoon sesame oil
    1/2 to 1 teaspoon garlic powder
    1/2 teaspoon salt

Cook bean sprouts in boiling water for 2 minutes. Drain and chop coarsely. Add ground beef, tofu, and 1 egg. Combine with Mixture A in a large bowl and mix well until it forms a ball. Place 1 teaspoonful of filling in open egg roll skin. Fold into a triangular shape, pinching edges together (may use water or mixed egg to seal seams of egg roll). Cook in boiling oil (about 375° F) for approximately 1 minute until

light brown. Drain excess oil on paper towel. Serve
hot. May be kept warm in the oven.

*Cucumber Pickles*

10 cucumbers
3 tablespoons salt
Stuffing Mixture:
    1/2 pound radish (Japanese white radish),
      cut into long, thin strips and squeezed dry
      (save juice for Mixture A)
    1 teaspoon cayenne pepper
    2 green onions, cut into long, thin strips
    1 teaspoon minced garlic
    1/2 teaspoon minced ginger
    1/2 dried chili pepper, finely shredded
Mixture A:
    1/2 cup radish juice
    3 cups water
    1 tablespoon salt
    1 1/2 teaspoons sugar

Rub cucumbers with salt and let them sit for a few
minutes. When they become soft, wash them, and cut
off their ends. Cut each cucumber in half, crosswise.
Then make 2-3 lengthwise slits in each piece, taking
care not to cut all the way through or to slice the ends.

Sprinkle the radish strips with cayenne pepper and let them stand 4-5 minutes. Combine them with the other stuffing items and mix well. Fill the slits in the cucumbers with this mixture.

Place the cucumbers alongside each other in an earthenware crock or a deep porcelain dish. Cover with a wooden lid or a plate small enough to fit inside crock and rest on cucumbers.

Pour Mixture A into crock. Cover and set in a warm place. If kept at 80-82° F., pickles will be ready in 2 days.

### *Korean Beef Patties*

1 pound very lean ground beef
4 tablespooons soy sauce
2 tablespoons sugar
1 tablespoon toasted, crushed sesame seeds
1 tablespoon sesame oil
2 1/2 tablespoons chopped green onion
1 tablespoon minced garlic
black pepper to taste

Mix all the items in the recipe together. Form the mixture into round balls and flatten them into patties. Broil the patties on the grill or bake them in a hot oven until done. Serves four.

Korean traditions concerning foods are changing. For many years, cooks served from five to fifteen side dishes at a meal. Today people do not think that such a wide selection is necessary. Modern Koreans have adopted foods from other nations, too. In Seoul, for instance, nearly everyone likes to buy ice cream cones.

Many other ideas about foods, clothes, houses, and furniture are changing in Korea. Two ideas remain the same in every home, though: the family is the most important part of one's life, and devotion to one's parents is the most important duty.

# 7. Education: The Korean Road to Success

Until modern times, there were only private schools in Korea. Old stories tell about parents who sacrificed everything—even food—so that their sons might attend these schools. Wealthy parents hired teachers for their sons, and these men prepared students for future government service. Confucian scholars or Buddhist monks held classes for those would could pay.

Unless the students wanted to become teachers or monks themselves, they hoped to enter government service. Because the tests for these jobs were very difficult, students had to work hard to pass them. They studied history, geography, science, and mathematics. Literature was important, too. The men who served kings—and even the kings themselves—often wrote poetry.

The Chinese influenced many of the Koreans' ideas about education. Because of the role China had played in their history, the Koreans felt that Chinese ideas were special. They studied Chinese history, culture, and literature, and they used the Chinese system of writing even though they spoke the Korean language. Educated persons had to learn to write thousands and thousands of Chinese characters.

After King Sejong invented Han'gŭl in the fifteenth century, the common people were easily able to learn to read and write Korean. Because the new alphabet was simple and easy to understand, everyone learned all the symbols in just a short time. Chinese writing was still used by the highly educated, but Han'gŭl was used by everyone.

As the years passed, some leaders were sorry that so many people were learning to read and write. They decided that written information could be a weapon as well as a tool, and they forbade the use of Han'gŭl. But the alphabet lived on, and more men and boys learned to read and write. Education for women was thought unnecessary, though, and there were no schools for people unable to pay.

When Korea opened its doors to the Western world in 1882, modern education entered. American missionaries started many fine schools within the country. In 1886 the first woman missionary, Mary F. Scranton, opened Korea's first school for girls in Seoul. She had only four students. Now called Ewha University and attended by more than 8,000 students, it is the world's largest school for educating women.

Today Korea has one of the world's best educated populations. But the story of modern education in Korea is not a tale of easy success. Over the past hundred years, many sad things have happened.

After Japan took control of Korea in 1910, education was limited again. The government allowed only the Japanese language to be taught in public, and only a small number of children were permitted to attend schools. The Japanese arrested some Korean teachers for teaching Han'gŭl, and they banned or destroyed anything that contained information about Korean history. They wanted the Koreans to forget their ancient heritage.

After World War II, when the country was divided, a terrible war broke out between the north and the south. Many schools in both halves of the country were closed or destroyed. In fact, during the three years of fighting, seven out of every ten elementary schools in Korea were damaged. Children had to attend classes in tents or in army barracks.

After peace was declared in 1953, the work of rebuilding Korea began. Most people felt that it had to start with education, which they believed lay at the base of a strong nation. In both the north and the south, schools were built, teachers were trained, and public schools were opened.

Today all children from six to twelve years of age receive a state-supported education in South Korea. In North Korea, state education begins when children are still babies. They can go to nursery schools which have been set up to help out working mothers.

Since the United States has close ties with the Republic of Korea, most information about Korean education comes from its half of the peninsula. Thousands of South Korean students are studying in colleges and universities in the United States, and thousands of American students are attending American schools in the Republic of Korea. As a result, ideas are easily shared.

People in the south freely admit that there are some problems in their schools, and they talk about ways to solve them. They are working to have smaller classes and better paid teachers.

Facts about schools in the Democratic People's Republic of Korea are harder to find. Few Americans have visited these schools, and no North Korean students are studying in the United States. Reports about education in North Korea come from government leaders rather than the students themselves, and many Westerners feel that not all the facts they present are true. Communist leaders say that there are no problems in their schools and that all students and teachers are satisfied and happy.

Even though the north and the south have different governments, some ideas about education are the same in both parts of Korea. There is a great respect for learning, and students obey their teachers because educators are honored persons. Since the people

*This picture shows a page from a textbook used by first graders in a South Korean primary school.*

believe that education can bring wealth and success, children are urged to study hard. Except for the hour they take for lunch, they work steadily at their lessons. Some students can go home for lunch, but most carry rice, kimch'i, or other favorite foods to school with them in metal containers. Books and papers are often carried in backpacks.

Schools are open six days a week, ten months a year. On Saturdays there are classes only half the day, but many students stay all day for special activities. There are weeks during both summer and winter when the schools are closed because the weather is very hot or very cold. Some schools in the south are not heated because of the high cost of fuel, and so children and teachers may wear coats during cold weather. Students laugh and say that gym becomes their favorite class then because they can jump around and keep warm. In the north, leaders say that all schools have steam heat.

Education in South Korea is divided into four stages: primary schools (first to sixth grades), middle schools (seventh to ninth grades), high schools (tenth to twelfth grades), and college-level schools. In the south, the government pays most of the cost of educating students for six years. Families must help pay school fees after the sixth grade, but educators hope to provide students with three more years of public schooling in the near future.

In the north, the government pays all schooling costs from the nursery level through the ninth grade. It may even pay all university costs for state-selected students. All students attend elementary school for grades one through four, and middle school for grades five through nine.

Class sizes differ from place to place. Because of a teacher shortage, the south's schools may have sixty to sixty-five students per teacher. Leaders in the north say that their classes are much smaller. Korean children often learn their lessons by repeating words in a chorus, and so a classroom may sometimes sound very noisy. Teachers expect students to memorize long lists of facts. They are often too busy to spend a lot of time with only one child, and so most students learn to help each other.

After sixth grade, boys and girls go to different classes or schools. For many years they wore special uniforms and hairstyles that showed their class rank, but this practice is no longer followed in the south. In 1982, Chun Doo Hwan, South Korea's president, said that students were free to wear whatever they wished to public schools.

Students your age spend thirty to thirty-one hours per week in the classroom. In the south these hours are spent in the following way: language study, six hours; arithmetic, five hours; social studies, four hours; nature classes, four hours; physical education, three hours; practical arts, three hours; moral education, two hours; music, two hours; and fine arts, two hours. As students move on to higher grades, they spend more time in the classroom. Seventh to ninth graders attend school thirty-two to thirty-five hours per week.

Classes in art, drama, and music are very important. In the north, all children play an instrument, starting in kindergarten. All over the peninsula, students learn many folk dances and patriotic songs. They learn to act in plays and often work with puppets. Calligraphy, a special form of writing, may be taught in art classes. Students in these classes learn

*Calligraphy, a beautiful form of writing, is sometimes taught in Korean students' art classes.*

to draw the letters of the alphabet by using special brushes and inks. Girls may learn flower arranging, and both boys and girls are taught to find beauty and art in nature.

Because Koreans feel that strong bodies are as necessary as clever minds, physical exercise is an important part of each school day. Children learn self-defense skills when they take part in games and sports.

Groups which meet after regular school hours become more and more important as students grow older. In the south, young people work for the National Movement for Spiritual Renewal, where they study ways to improve life in their nation. Middle school and high school students march in parades and help in their communities. In the north, primary students belong to the Young Pioneers, and they later join the Socialist Working Youth League. Belonging to after-school groups is as necessary as studying lessons during school hours. Students are taught how to behave and to serve their country.

Homework is given by all teachers. The higher the grade, the more difficult the work. In order to go on to high school, middle school students must pass a test. Since only the very best students are accepted, parents want their children to do well. As the day of school examinations gets closer, they worry more and more. Fortune-tellers in Seoul say that a common question people ask about their future is, "Will my child do well on the school examination?"

Students may take an academic course, which leads to college, or a vocational course, which helps them get jobs. The tests to get into college are the hardest part of all, and only the top students are able to attend. In the north, it is a very great honor to be chosen to attend Kim Il Sung University in P'yŏng-yang.

All over the peninsula young men must serve in the armed forces once their schooling is finished, and so they work hard to get the best education possible. Those who earn the best marks may be trained as officers.

As you can see, the two Koreas continue to share a love of learning despite their differences. More and more schools are being opened for deaf, blind, and mentally or physically handicapped people, and more and more adult education classes are being offered. Most people in both the north and the south believe that success can come if everyone works and studies hard. Education is a very important part of life for all Koreans, and they hope to keep improving their schools as the years go by.

# 8. *International Fun: Games and Sports*

When a group of Korean children are seen gathered together in a schoolyard, they may be playing a game exactly like one you know. You could join right in because no words are needed to show who is the winner and who is the loser.

We call the game paper, scissors, rock; the Koreans call it *kawi bawi bo.* But their rules are the same as ours. Players must use one of their hands to make a sign for each object—a flat hand for paper, a fist for rock, and two fingers for scissors. Then at a set signal, they must make one of the three signs, or symbols. The player with the strongest symbol showing is the winner. The rock beats the scissors, the scissors cut the paper, and the paper covers the rock.

Sometimes Korean schoolchildren use this game to determine who goes first in other games. The winner gets to have first choice.

Another game you could join in is blind man's buff, for again, no words are needed, and the rules are the same all over the world. A blindfolded "it" must catch and identify all the other players.

These games, and other similar ones, have been popular in Korea for centuries because no expensive equipment is needed to play them. Korea was a poor nation for many years, and so its people learned to find entertainment by using whatever material they had at home. They made dolls for girls from straw stalks, and whistles for boys from poplar bark.

As a result of Korea's recent economic success, games and toys can now be bought in stores. The sports and game shops the Koreans have look almost exactly like the ones you know about. Perhaps some of the balls, gloves, skates, or jogging shoes you use now were made in Korea just a few months ago.

Still, many Koreans feel that the best entertainment is the free kind that can be enjoyed at home. Like their ancient ancestors, they take pleasure in gathering with their families in the evening and exchanging riddles and stories. "When you whittle with a knife, what can you make which will grow larger as you work?" an elder brother might ask. And everyone will laugh because the young ones cannot come up with the answer—a hole.

Other games the Koreans enjoy at home require some type of equipment. *Yut* is the most popular because it can be played by both adults and children. This game consists of four sticks and a board. The players use the sticks much like we use dice, tossing them into the air to see how many movements they are allowed to make on the yut board.

*Yut, a board game, is played by tossing sticks into the air. How the sticks land determines the game's outcome.*

Since the sticks are round on one side and flat on the other, they can land in five different positions. Players want the sticks to land flat side up so that they can move more quickly across the board. Yut is similar to Parcheesi, except for the movements that can be made on the board.

*Hwato*, another very popular game, is played with forty-eight flower cards divided into twelve suits. Each suit stands for one month of the year, and every card shows some type of flower or shrub.

Hwato rules are similar to those of a card game you might play—rummy. The object of the game is to form matched sets of cards. When players have cards that match, they lay them on the table. Since each suit has a certain value, the player with the most valuable sets wins the game.

People sometimes gamble when they play this game, and the winner receives money for each point. Children's games don't involve much money, but adults may decide to take the winner out to dinner and a movie. Card games like hwato are played by people of all ages in Korea. They can take place any time, even when groups of people are gathered together to mourn the death of a friend.

*Paduk*, which was invented by the Chinese centuries ago, is another popular game. It is played on a checkerboard by two people. The older of the two uses white pieces, the younger, black ones. Each player tries to win more territory on the board by surrounding the other player's pieces. The rules of the game are more complicated than those for chess.

Because paduk takes so much thought and skill, the Koreans say it is more of an art than a game. They have set up paduk parlors in many cities so that people can watch skillful players. Many newspapers print paduk problems, and they offer prizes to readers who can solve them.

*Hiking in the mountains is an activity that almost all Koreans enjoy.*

Other recreational activities require physical skill. Again, the oldest and most popular ones are those which cost little to take part in. Almost all Koreans like to hike, and many families spend their free time on mountain trails. Since Korea is so hilly, a good hike in an open area is only minutes away from most cities. At the top of some of the highest peaks, special medals are given to the climbers. Many Buddhist temples are hidden high in the hills, and believers often spend many hours hiking to visit them.

Perhaps because so many Korean children enjoy

hiking, Korea has produced some of the world's best mountain climbers. Professionals from the Republic of Korea thrilled the whole world in 1977 when Ko Sang-don and his team scaled Mount Everest, the highest peak on earth. This group was the thirteenth team to reach the top.

The hills and mountains of Korea encourage another popular family sport—skiing. The north has long winters, so the skiing season there lasts many months. New snow-making machines have increased the season in the south to four months. Dragon Valley is South Korea's best known ski area, and skiers there have the latest equipment. In rural areas children often make their own winter sports equipment. Outgrown ice skates, for instance, can be hammered on a board to make a fine sled.

Koreans are world experts in another sport which they practice all year around. It, too, requires little money. Over 2,000 years ago they developed ways of defending themselves in which they used only their hands and feet. According to old military records, the Yi kingdom had more than one hundred different names for this no-weapon or empty-hand fighting. These various methods of self-defense were divided into three classes: those which would stun an enemy, those which would knock an enemy unconscious, and those which would kill.

*South Korea's Dragon Valley is a popular place for skiing and
snowmobiling.*

*Korean youngsters who take part in t'aekwŏndo contests try to break small boards with their hands and feet.*

In the past, soldiers used these methods to protect themselves or to attack their enemies. But after they began wearing armor, they could no longer move fast enough to use these ways of fighting in battle. Korean men gave up using them in war and began studying and practicing them for sport.

Today Koreans are world famous for *t'ae-kwŏndo*, a form of combat in which fighters battle each other with their hands and feet. *T'ae* means "to smash with the feet," *kwŏn* means "destroying with the hand or fist," and *do* means "method."

T'aekwŏndo schools have been set up throughout Korea. The students who attend them are taught how the mind and the body work together, as well as how to breathe in a certain way. There are special classes for children and for adults. Points in the sport are given for correct actions and movements.

People all over the world have become interested in Korean t'aekwŏndo. More than a thousand Koreans are teaching the skills of the sport to people in over eighty countries. Women, too, are becoming experts. In 1977 the sport's world championship matches were held in Chicago, and now many American cities offer t'aekwŏndo classes for both adults and children. Perhaps you or your friends have taken these classes.

Korean wrestling also has a long history. Centuries ago soldiers used it for physical training; today it is a national sport. The object of the sport is for one wrestler to throw another off balance by using only body movements. No striking is allowed. The wrestler who touches the ground with any part of his body other than his feet loses the match.

In 1882, when Western ideas entered Korea, the people there were introduced to many new sports. They learned to play and enjoy baseball, basketball, soccer, tennis, track, gymnastics, horse racing, and golf. Although they had taken part in some form of these sports in villages for centuries, they learned international rules and began forming professional teams to play in national events.

Today soccer is the most popular outdoor game in both the north and the south. Children in schools play on all-girl or all-boy teams, and they compete within their cities or villages. The Republic of Korea sends top-rated high school teams to compete in Japan. It also has professional teams that play in huge stadiums. Korean children admire soccer stars the way Americans admire baseball heroes. Baseball and basketball are gaining in popularity among Koreans, but soccer games attract the biggest crowds.

Like people from other nations, Koreans strive to win Olympic medals in global competition. Because of their country's division, however, the two Koreas have not been able to enter many of the same events. Often the government of South Korea and the government of North Korea refuse to allow their athletes to compete with each other. In 1988 the Summer Olympic Games will be held in Seoul. South Korea's president, Chun Doo Hwan, has stated that his government will welcome all Olympic athletes, whatever their political viewpoint.

The first Olympic medal the Republic of Korea ever won was for volleyball. In 1976 its women's team captured a bronze medal in Canada. Korean women have also been outstanding as pingpong champions, often appearing in the world finals.

The Democratic People's Republic of Korea has

a number of excellent pingpong players, too. In fact, the country opened its doors to the rest of the world partly because of its pride in their ability. In 1979 it hosted the world table tennis championship in P'yŏng-yang. Nine hundred players from seventy countries took part. Because of government problems, Korean players from the south did not attend, but the United States sent a team. Americans were happy to have a chance to visit a place which had been closed to them for nearly thirty years.

The biggest international athletic event in Korea's 5,000 year history took place in Seoul in 1978. Fifteen hundred people from seventy-one countries took part in a world shooting championship. The stadium was mobbed with fans from all over the world, and the flags from all their nations flew high over the crowds.

Some people feel that sports and games between nations are the path to peace for the future. They believe that when men and women compete on the playing field instead of the battlefield, they make the world a better place. With their love of sports and games, the Koreans are eager for international contests. They know that there are no losers in this kind of competition because everyone can enjoy watching or playing the games.

# 9. *The Koreans Who Became Americans*

Throughout their long history, few Koreans ever traveled far from their homes. Even though they suffered hardships because of war or cruel leaders, most of them wanted to remain in Korea. Because of their strong family ties and their duty to honor the memory of their ancestors, they wanted to stay close to the place where they had been born.

Since 1900, however, thousands of Koreans have come to the United States. Between 1902 and 1905 many men left their homeland to find jobs in Hawaii. In 1905 people who wanted to escape the Japanese government began leaving for America. They continued coming until the end of World War II in 1945. Between 1945 and 1950 a few women were allowed to leave the country in order to marry Korean men already in the United States. So, too, were a number of students who wanted to attend American schools. Finally, a great many people fled to the United States when war broke out between North and South Korea in 1950.

People decide to leave, or emigrate from, their country for many different reasons. In 1901 the weather in Korea played a part in forcing some people to leave. First there was a long dry spell, followed by sudden rains that caused great flooding. The rice crops were ruined, and many people faced starvation.

At the same time, Hawaiian plantation owners asked for Korean workers to help in the sugar fields. The owners said they would pay all travel expenses and fifteen dollars per month to each worker. The working conditions would be difficult—ten hours a day, six days a week, under a hot sun—but to some Koreans without food, money, or a job the idea sounded good.

Christian missionaries in Korea urged some of their church members to leave for Hawaii as soon as possible. They believed that Korean Christians would be happier in a Christian nation, and they thought that the job offers were good opportunities for the workers.

King Kojong's government, which was under the control of the Japanese, did not like having people leave Korea, but it finally allowed some workers to go. Before emigration was forbidden in 1905, almost 7,000 workers had arrived in Hawaii. Many of them either stayed there after their work contract was finished or moved on to California.

These early pioneers on the plantations struggled not to become like Westerners. Mothers told their sons not to wear tight trousers or eat strange foods.

Many workers tried to wear Korean hairstyles, hats, and clothing in Hawaii. But they usually cut off their long hair within ten days of their arrival, and they began wearing simple plantation clothing, which was safer near the sugar-making machinery.

The workers missed having Korean food. But unless they paid special wages to a cook, they had to eat the same food that was served to Chinese and Japanese workers. Often the Koreans banded together to pay the extra money in order to eat foods from their homeland.

Language was also a difficulty for the Koreans. Some workers died because they could not explain their illness to doctors who spoke only English. One worker told a researcher many years later that the Koreans worked like animals and suffered terrible treatment. They could not complain, though, he said, because they did not know the language.

Then, too, many of the workers were lonely. Since ninety percent of them were men and only ten percent were women, most of the men were unable to find Korean wives. To deal with this problem a "picture bride" system was begun. Under this system, the men were allowed to send their pictures back to Korea. If a woman was willing to marry, she then left Korea on a special passport, and the couple was married on the dock where her ship landed.

Between 1910 and 1924 more than eight hundred brides went to Hawaii, and more than one hundred went on to the mainland. But not all of them found happiness. Sometimes the picture brides were shocked to see that their bridegrooms were much older and uglier than the pictures they had sent. Some brides were only fifteen, and many grooms were well over forty. A few young women fainted at the sight of their future husbands, and several refused to leave the ships which had brought them. Those who did marry, however, became a stable base for future Korean communities in America.

The years from 1905 to 1950 are called the "semi-official" years for Korean emigrants because many people left for America without official passports or permission. The picture brides were one example — they had to marry before leaving the docks so that they could use their husbands' passports.

Another group were the Koreans protesting Japanese rule in Korea. Some escaped the Japanese secret police by going north, disguising themselves as Chinese and departing from China. Several hundred of these political refugees — who had no passports — were admitted to the United States under a special ruling.

Some Korean students were permitted to enter the United States for educational purposes, and a few of them were able to stay permanently. Christian missionaries still living in Korea helped a number of young people enter colleges and universities in America. But this group was not large. Official records state that less than 900 students had entered the country by the year 1940.

In these early decades of the twentieth century, definite types of Koreans were emigrating to Hawaii or the mainland: plantation workers, picture brides, political refugees, and students. These people, so different in background and education, found that their Korean heritage bound them together. In California they formed three kinds of organizations to help each other: community groups to help in daily life; churches and schools for religion and education; and political groups to speak out for freeing Korea.

Some writers call the Koreans in America during these years the "forgotten people" because there were so few of them compared to the Chinese or Japanese. During the first half of this century, there were never more than 10,000 Koreans in America at any one time. Loneliness, hardship, and weariness marked their lives. In many ways they were people without a country, since they had rejected the government in Korea, and the government in the United States seemed to ignore them. Often even the best educated had to settle for back-breaking, low-paying jobs.

A wave of bad feeling against Asian immigrants was sweeping over the United States in these early decades, too, because these people were willing to work for such low pay. White workers talked about the "yellow peril," and they said that the immigrants should not be given jobs. Farmers in California banded together and stormed fruit farms which had hired Koreans.

One American, Mrs. Mary E. Steward of Upland, California, bravely stood up for her Korean workers against the rioters. She said that they were hard-working, earnest, honest people who were struggling for a decent life. But not enough people shared her ideas. In 1924 the U.S. Congress passed the Oriental Exclusion Act, and no more Koreans were allowed to enter America except to attend colleges and universities.

Those Koreans who were in America tried even harder to become successful. In California, fruit pickers dreamed of owning their own business. Two brothers were trying to develop a new fruit—a fuzzless peach. When their nectarine was ready for market, it was highly praised. Later, the Kim Company became a multimillion dollar business.

Other Koreans had political dreams. Syngman Rhee was a Korean student who studied in America. He often spoke out against the rule of the Japanese government. Many years later, in 1948, he became the first president of the Republic of Korea.

There were many small business success stories, too. Koreans became experts at family-owned barber, laundry, fruit, or vegetable shops. The first generation immigrants worked hard and made certain that their many children were well educated. Because of this, the second generation Koreans quickly learned English and adapted to the American style of life.

When Japan attacked Hawaii in 1941, America quickly took steps to defend itself against that country. Thousands of Japanese people in the United States were sent to special camps. Some Koreans were sent there, too, simply because they looked like Japanese citizens.

Koreans who were not sent to the camps suffered insults all through World War II. When the war ended and Korea was divided, most Americans didn't know or care what was happening there.

Then in 1950, when war broke out in Korea, everyone in the United States heard about the divided peninsula. Thousands of American soldiers were sent there to fight, and nearly thirty-four thousand of them died in battle. After peace talks began, the government in the south agreed that the U.S. military forces should remain. Korea then became a regular duty station for American soldiers.

After the war, a number of people left Korea again. They were all from South Korea, however, because emigration from North Korea was forbidden in 1945. Most of these South Koreans were women who had married American soldiers. They were called "war brides," and some of them brought young children with them.

In 1954 American adoption agencies entered South Korea, and a second new type of emigration began. Because of the war, there were many homeless children in the land. Orphans with no families or food roamed the streets. There were abandoned babies, too, because some soldiers fathered children and then left the country. The South Korean women, left alone, could not feed or support children without a father. According to Confucian thinking, children exist only if their father is present to claim them. As a result, South Korean children without a legal father could not get an education or find work.

Because of this situation, American agencies helped send small children to new families in the United States. Laws had to be changed so that they could become immigrants. Many of these children without two Korean parents are still arriving today. Recently, though, the South Korean government has stated that by 1985 all children born in that country will be cared for in their homeland.

Korean immigrants have also enriched American family life. A great many of them have become part of American families through marriage, and thousands more through adoption.

Good things can happen for everyone when people from many nations can live together in peace. Today the United States and the Korean immigrants are working together to make a better life for all.

# Appendix A

# Korean Consulates in the United States and Canada

The Korean consulates in the United States and Canada want to help North Americans understand Korean ways. For information about Korea, contact the consulate or embassy nearest you.

## U. S. Consulates

*Atlanta, Georgia*
Korean Consulate General
Harris Tower
233 Peachtree Street
Atlanta, Georgia  30303
Phone (404) 522-1611

*Chicago, Illinois*
Korean Consulate General
500 North Michigan Avenue
Chicago, Illinois  60611
Phone (312) 822-9485

*Houston, Texas*
Korean Consulate General
1520 Texas Avenue, Suite 802
Houston, Texas  77002
Phone (713) 227-4205

*Los Angeles, California*
Korean Consulate General
5455 Wilshire Boulevard, Suite 1101
Los Angeles, California  90036
Phone (213) 931-1331

*New York, New York*
Korean Consulate General
460 Park Avenue, Sixth Floor
New York, New York  10022
Phone (212) 752-1700

*San Francisco, California*
Korean Consulate General
3500 Clay Street
San Francisco, California 94118
Phone (415) 921-2252

*Washington, D.C.*
Embassy of Korea
2370 Massachusetts Avenue NW
Washington, D.C.  20008
Phone (202) 483-7383

**Canadian Consulates**

*Montreal, Quebec*
    Korean Consulate General
    1000 Sherbrooke Street West, Suite 2205
    Montreal, Quebec  H3A 2P2
    Phone (514) 845-3243

*Ottawa, Ontario*
    Embassy of Korea
    151 Slater Street, Suite 608
    Ottawa, Ontario  K1P 5H3
    Phone (613) 232-1715

*Toronto, Ontario*
    Korean Consulate General
    439 University Avenue, Suite 700
    Toronto, Ontario  M5G 1Y8
    Phone (416) 598-4608

*Vancouver, British Columbia*
    Korean Consulate General
    1066 Hastings Street West, Suite 830
    Vancouver, British Columbia  V6E 3X1
    Phone (604) 681-9581

**Other Sources of Information**

Information Center on Children's Culture
331 East Thirty-eighth Street
New York, New York  10016

Korean Cultural Service
5505 Wilshire Boulevard
Los Angeles, California  90036

Korea National Tourism Corporation
Chicago Office
230 North Michigan Avenue, Suite 1500
Chicago, Illinois  60601

## *Appendix B*

## *Pronouncing Korean Words*

Various methods have been developed to represent Korean words in English. The words in this book are transcribed according to the McCune-Reischauer system, the one most widely used in the United States.

The symbols of the Korean alphabet (Han'gŭl) and their approximate equivalent sounds in English are shown on p. 137. As the chart indicates, some consonants have more than one sound, depending on whether they appear at the beginning, middle, or end of a word. The letter ㄱ , for example, is pronounced as a *k* at the beginning and end of a word, and a *g* in the middle of one.

Because the position of a consonant determines its pronunciation, certain words are not said the way they are spelled. For example, the sound [s] cannot be pronounced at the end of a word even though some words end in *s*. Likewise, forms which are based on the verb stem *pis-* (" to comb"), are spelled *pis-ŏ* and *pis-ko*, but pronounced as [pisŏ] and [pikko].

As you can see, the Korean language has a complex sound system. That is why scholars have a difficult time representing it in English.

## ...VELS

**...VOWELS ARE
...XT TO THE
...S**

| SYMBOL | SOUNDS LIKE | |
|---|---|---|
| | $a$ | (f*a*ther) |
| | $ya$ | (y*a*cht) |
| | $ŏ$ | (*o*nion) |
| | $yŏ$ | (y*ou*ng) |
| | $i$ | (mar*i*ne) |

ㅁ — $m$

ㄴ — $n$

ㅇ — Silent before vowel; *ng* in middle or at end of word

ㅍ — $p$

ㄹ — $t, l$

ㅅ — $s$

ㅌ — $t$

## THESE FIVE VOWELS ARE WRITTEN UNDER THE CONSONANTS

| SYMBOL | SOUNDS LIKE | |
|---|---|---|
| ㅗ | $o$ | (*o*ld) |
| ㅛ | $yo$ | (y*o*del) |
| ㅜ | $oo$ | (sp*oo*k) |
| ㅠ | $yu$ | (y*u*le) |
| ― | $ŭ$ | (*u*tter) |

# *Glossary*

**abŏji**—father

**celadon**—a special kind of Korean pottery

**chiggehs**—a large wooden backpack

**chip**—family home

**Ch'usŏk**—a holiday similar to Thanksgiving

**halmŏni**—grandmother

**Han'gŭl**—the Korean alphabet

**harabŏji**—grandfather

**Honored Dead**—the name Koreans give to their ancestors

**Hwan'gap**—a sixtieth birthday party

**kawi bawi bo**—a Korean game similar to the Western game of paper, scissors, rock

**kimch'i**—a highly spiced vegetable dish

**ŏmŏni**—mother

**ondol**—a heating method in which hot air from an indoor fireplace is carried to other parts of a house by means of pipes located under its floors

**paduk**—a game played on a board, using white and black stones

**ramyon**—flavored noodles

**shaman**—a person who is believed to be able to influence spirits

**t'aekwŏndo**—a form of combat in which fighters battle each other with their hands and feet

**Tano**—a holiday celebrated in the spring

**yoboseyo**—a word of address commonly used with both strangers and friends
**yong**—dragon
**yut**—a game played on a board, using sticks

# *Selected Bibliography*

Berrean, Sally. *City of Seoul*. Seoul, Korea: Kaeyang Printing Co., 1977.

Carpenter, Frances. *Tales of a Korean Grandmother*. Tokyo, Japan: Charles E. Tuttle Co., 1976.

Draeger, Donn F., and Smith, Robert W. *Comprehensive Asian Fighting Arts*. New York: Kodansha International, 1980.

Ferrar, G. K. *Mr. Hong and the Dragon, and Other Korean Stories*. Seoul, Korea: Royal Asiatic Society, 1975.

Hyung, Peter, ed. *It's Fun Being Young in Korea*. Seoul, Korea: Samhwa Printing Co., 1980.

Johnston, Richard J. H. *Getting to Know the Two Koreas*. New York: Coward-McCann, 1965.

Kim, Hyung-chan, and Patterson, Wayne. *The Koreans in America*. Minneapolis: Lerner Publications Co., 1977.

Korean Overseas Information Service. *A Handbook of Korea, 1982*. Seoul, Korea: 1981.

Solberg, S. E. *The Land and People of Korea*. New York: J. B. Lippincott Co., 1973.

Tor, Regina. *Getting to Know Korea*. New York: Coward-McCann, 1953.

Yoon, Suk-Joong. *Half Past Four*. Los Angeles: F. T. Yoon Co., 1978.

# Index

## About the Author

Free-lance writer Carol Farley has a great affection for Korea and its people. From 1977 to 1979 she lived in Seoul, Korea, where she taught at several schools, including Hanyang University. This experience later prompted her to write *Korea: A Land Divided.*

Author of fourteen other books for young people, Ms. Farley has won several awards for her writing. In 1976 the Child Study Association named *The Garden Is Doing Fine* as its Best Book of the Year. Another story, *Loosen Your Ears*, was named Best Book by a Midwest Writer by the Friends of the Writer in 1978.

Ms. Farley and her family live in Mount Pleasant, Michigan. She currently serves on the board of directors of the Society of Children's Book Writers. In addition, she has recently completed work on a master's degree in children's literature at Central Michigan University.